BEYOND BELIEF

BEYOND BELIEF

LIVING INTO SPIRITUAL INTELLIGENCE

Timothy Thorstenson

RESOURCE *Publications* · Eugene, Oregon

BEYOND BELIEF
Living into Spiritual Intelligence

Resource Publications
An Imprint of Wipf and Stock Publishers
199 W. 8th Ave., Suite 3
Eugene, OR 97401

www.wipfandstock.com

PAPERBACK ISBN: 978-1-6667-3284-9
HARDCOVER ISBN: 978-1-6667-2698-5
EBOOK ISBN: 978-1-6667-2699-2

.   NOVEMBER 1, 2021 11:16 AM

For all my patients,
who taught me, by their gentle example,
how to live with courage and hope;
For all my nurse and physician colleagues,
for their kindness and commitment;
For all my students,
for their trust and open hearts;
For Oz and Mark and Max,
for Ruth and David,
for their guidance and encouragement;
For Gail and Maren and Karli,
for their love and support.

Every happening great and small is a parable whereby God speaks to us, and the art of life is to get the message.

—MALCOLM MUGGERIDGE

The most beautiful thing we can experience is the Mysterious.

—ALBERT EINSTEIN

Contents

Acknowledgements

Thank you to Susan M. Jones, neuroscientist and research assistant extraordinaire, without whom I would not have completed this book.

Thank you to Gail Gentling, public health professional and spouse, for suggested edits, wise comments, heart-felt reflections, ongoing support— and for improving my writing in every way.

Introduction

THESE ARE CHALLENGING AND FASCINATING DAYS. You may have found, like me, that maintaining a grounded sense of personal spirituality and growing spiritual intelligence is a challenge, living as we are in a land that is actively wrestling with its history and its divisions and its future. If you are finding yourself feeling anxious or frustrated or discouraged about the state of things in America and the world today, you are certainly not alone. Indeed, most people who have been attuned to recent political, social and environmental dynamics at play are experiencing significant emotional distress. Our lifestyles, our values, our very lives, have been under duress and threat. We would simply be out of touch to claim that all is well in the face of all that is unfolding. Given the pandemic and the political schisms, it is a painful and troubling time for all of us, no matter our religious or cultural beliefs.

Yet it is also one filled with potential for new ways of being and for expanding our perspectives on what makes for a meaningful life. As the fabric of our society has been fraying and as faith in our institutions has been sorely tested, a counter-narrative has also been unfolding. New social movements are rising up, thoughtful and reflective people are becoming politically engaged as never before, and society is slowing waking up to the need for significant social and economic change. It may even be that we are entering into a time of significant transition and a kind of spiritual renewal that will lead us to greater courage, greater participation, greater collaboration and deeper learning, though that, of course, remains uncertain since it always comes at a cost.

It was the Italian philosopher Antonio Gramsi who famously said, "The old world is dying, and the new world struggles to be born: now is the time of monsters."[1] And there are monsters indeed, many of them clothed in the costumes of nationalism, racism and religious righteousness. Extremist leaders in both state and national governments are introducing legislation to constrict immigration, human rights, and voting rights, all in the effort to preserve white dominance and the status quo. Social media is rife with divisive opinions and culture wars on most every social issue, from mask wearing in schools to the emotional wellbeing of Olympic athletes to the latest conspiracy theory. Meanwhile, according to the latest census data, America is becoming increasingly secular and non-white, while conservative evangelical church members continue their drift toward far-right positions. And perhaps most significantly, young black men are still being killed by increasingly militarized police, in an epidemic of white privilege and power.

In the three weeks of testimony in the Derek Chauvin trial (the police officer who knelt on the neck of George Floyd, causing his death), sixty-four people across the country died at the hands of police, more than half of them Black and Latino, including a nineteen-year-old just ten miles from where the Chauvin trial was held in Minneapolis, and a thirteen-year-old boy in Chicago. And it is not lost on thoughtful observers that the common thread among the great majority of mass murderers of the last ten years is that they have been white Christian men with Anglo-Saxon last names. The same is true of those who assaulted the US Capitol Building on January 6th, 2021. It is fair to say that America is currently spiritually ill, suffering from the effects of its inability to overcome its racist past and its economic disparities, and from failing to honor its creeds and commitments. There are monsters aplenty. People in power the world over, and not least here in the United States, have sought to strengthen their holds on power, abusing whatever institutions (a free press, voting rights, guarantees of equality) or voices of resistance lie in their way. The world as a whole seems to be groaning in pain, as we face the harsh realities of a warming climate, a devastating pandemic, growing poverty and famine, and mass migration.

But for the most part, our institutions protecting human rights and democratic freedoms are holding, if just barely. It is a time of monsters, but we might also see it as a time for hope, as new collaborations and new partnerships are beginning to take hold, fueled by rapid communication across the internet. Whatever the future has in store for us, taking in and thinking about all the challenging and stimulating information and then

1. Gramsi, *Selections From The Prison Notebooks*, 275

engaging proactively in trying to better society is certainly energizing—and it is generating renewed optimism. The emphases on personal and social spirituality and on promoting human rights and global justice for all is enhancing life for many and making life more meaningful. At this early stage, it is generating a certain anticipation and hope, if not always contentment and equanimity.

Becoming more spiritually *intelligent* is the key that unlocks that more hopeful future, and in this book we will walk through that multifaceted process. To become more spiritually intelligent is to both enhance opportunities for collaboration and social advancement, and to increase a sense of purpose and meaning and personal contentment. As we study human history, it appears to be the essential developmental evolutionary trait that gives rise to hope. We are a hopeful people. And as a result, we are a people oriented toward ongoing learning and development, always in the process of becoming more than we have been. But the converse is also true unfortunately; that when our spiritual natures are injured or repressed or just not nurtured, we do less well, devolving into anxiety, despair, exclusive thinking, and ultimately abuse and violence. So we start with learning, that is, with becoming more astute about human history and about religious expression and about humankind's ongoing efforts to survive and get along and make sense of things. And then we want to become more astute about and attuned to what the term *spirituality* actually references—the energy in the universe and the life blood that animates us and generates our thoughts and feelings and our ideas and expressions, what some would call the divine spirit that generates life itself. And we want to work to make sense out of all that, out of all that is happening in our physical reality, working to discern what is moral and good and loving as we go, learning how to interact with our reality in meaningful ways. In that sense, becoming more spiritually intelligent is about both engaging what we are observing and experiencing and then reflecting on those observations to gain deepened self-understanding and deepened awareness about how our minds and our consciousness are shaped and influenced by that which flows around us and into us.

Developing greater spiritual intelligence, then, is about paying attention to what we observe and see and read, but so also is it about taking in and thinking about the inklings and insights and energy and motivation and inspiration that seems to well up within us as if prompted by an unknown and unseen spirit. Spiritual intelligence turns on learning and discerning enough about the energies and mysteries of life that we can align with them, with intentionality and mindfulness. To become more spiritually alive and attuned, we turn *purposely* toward that which animates us and encourages us and prompts our feelings and generates our hope and courage, even as we absorb all the stimuli of our actual lived experiences and of the events that confront us every day, so much of what today—on the surface, at least—is painful and frightening.

This book, then, will focus not only on making sense out of reality, but also on making sense out of our ongoing and eons-old efforts to perceive and interpret the movement of the divine, whatever that is. I orient toward a common sense spirituality, one that reflects what we have learned over time and one that is based in science and grounded in what we have and currently *are* learning. We will try to get at the nature and energy of the universe and of we call "the divine spirit," and we will reflect on the inherent meaning in religious expression and the nature of faith and the process of continually becoming more than we are.

Humankind is on a constant journey of *becoming*, that is, of exploration, discovery, reflection, and renewed perspective. As a person of an emerging and renewed sense of connection with that divine spirit, I myself have come to appreciate that journey, and the ever-growing, ever-deepening spirituality that feeds my soul. Indeed, the quest for understanding the nature of the divine and of our connections with the mysteries of what we refer to as "God," remains at the heart of what gives meaning to our lives.

No wonder we tend to lock-in our childhood definitions and hold tightly to our conclusions about that God, even when it becomes counterproductive and self-limiting or, worse, socially exclusive and even destructive. It is an age-old struggle. Humankind has always imagined and constructed gods and religions in attempts to understand the unknowable and the mystical, and to create meaning out of lived experience. We have long posited theological theories and made conclusive pronouncements in an effort to express our moral perspectives and to give voice to that sense of awe and mystery and connection with something greater, to what we can only perceive partially, and then only dimly, as if through dark glasses. Humankind has long sought to become more spiritually aware and attuned, and to better understand the "how-s and why-s" of our world, and the "why me-s?" and the "what now-s?" of our individual lives. It has been a worthy and rich process, if also inadequate and incomplete. And now we are moving rapidly beyond our constrained beliefs and limited knowledge, as the universe opens up to us in previously unimaginable ways. We see more today, both outward into the universe and downward into the quantum world, than we ever thought possible. Yet the question remains: how do we conceptualize what is not clearly capture-able, what is not fully definable, what is not totally visible? To more fully understand that which is hidden remains a human aspiration. Indeed, that quest may be more important today than ever as we face significant threats to our environment and well-being.

A key factor in this ancient journey into sacred reflection is the unlocking of science over the last several hundred years, but particularly in the last fifty years or so. It is curious that the battles fought in the late middle ages between the Roman Catholic Church and those engaged in scientific exploration have seen something of a reprise in these last many years, as scientific conclusions and fact-finding research have often been branded "fake news" by those who perceived them as threats to power or autonomy, not the least of which are the right wing evangelical churches, at least those that seem to have moved away from their core message toward politically-aligned moralism. That may merely be one of the monsters with which we need to contend during this time of rebirth as we discover that both astrophysics and quantum physics are helping to unlock spiritual mysteries and deepen our connection to the "Holy Other." Indeed, making sense of things and becoming more spiritually intelligent may turn on bringing science and theology into the same lifeboat, as we work to find ways to heal our world, and both prolong and transform our species.

Becoming more spiritually intelligent invites exploration into the many components that make up human perception. Becoming well informed and engaged with history—with the history of human development and social expression, with the evolution of religious movements and the invention of written scriptures, and with the progressive development of science that informs our process of becoming—is certainly an essential component of becoming more spiritually astute. So is exploring the sociology of our development, the psychology of it, and the science of it. And then it is about seeking to understand the nature of reality and figuring out how to live in harmony with it. In that sense, spiritual intelligence is all about *learning*, and about better understanding and expanding what consciousness actually is, what the energy is that flows through us and how it cues our thoughts and feelings. And it is about gaining ever greater insight and slowly becoming more attuned to the values and dynamics that give our lives meaning as well. Finally, it is about living with a hope based on deepened perceptivity and broadened insight and, yes, expanded faith—or perhaps better put, informed *trust*—trust in the unfolding of creation, in the creative movement of the universe's energy, in the beauty and wonder and transformative power of love.

Such has been my personal and professional journey, and this lived experience informs these reflections more than anything else; we make meaning by what we experience, by what we perceive, and by what we learn along the way. I hope that my experiences and learning will prompt a parallel reflection in the reader and an eagerness to continually expand consciousness and deepen connections with one another as well—and with whatever that divine spirit *is* that prompts the continuing unfolding.

❀❀❀❀❀

A bit of context: I grew up in a typically white, middle class family in the upper Midwest. My parents were third-generation Scandinavians by heritage, and thus ensconced in the Lutheran religious traditions. My grandfather had been a parish pastor in North Dakota, and two of his sons followed in his footsteps. His only daughter (out of eight children) was my mother, who was deeply engrained in traditional female roles. She was a stay-at-home mom, and we never wanted for good meals and had an abiding sense of security. My father was a straight-ahead civil engineer, a stoic, and an Eisenhower moderate republican. We fit the mold of industrious, independent, quiet, church-going Minnesotans, with a high value on education and personal responsibility. It made for something of a self-contained and very pleasant world.

But not all was well. The shadow side of our idealized lives played out for me in the silent exclusivity and conformity and mild repression. I was confined within a fairly tight culture, one that provided ample personal security but that also felt constraining. Over time, I slowly grew in my desire to break out. I sought deeper insight and understanding, I wanted more, I wanted to move beyond my felt anxiety and inadequacy and somehow "break free," though I had no idea what that might look like. I experienced the deeply-rooted Scandinavian culture of shame and of "not thinking too highly of ourselves" as mildly diminishing and controlling, and as the 1960s began to break things open, I wanted to explore it—and learn to understand it—all.

The happenstance of my birth in 1950 and the coming of age in the sixties was clearly a key factor. I was a teenager during that tumultuous and exciting decade, the youngest of three, and just coming into adolescence when President Kennedy was assassinated. I turned fourteen just as the Beatles arrived in the US, bringing with them a powerfully stimulating and transcendent way of being. The Civil Rights struggle and the war in Viet Nam were dominating the news, and society was experiencing the growing unrest of rapid economic development, tense international relations, and deeply troubling racism and poverty, and I was pulled in by all of it. I, like so many of my peers, was trying to figure out where I lined up and who I was becoming. For me as curious teenager, matters of identity, of faith, of sexuality and peer pressure and alcohol use, were all set against the larger issues of social unrest, the protest movement, and rock 'n' roll. And soon I would be facing going off to college, having to come to grips with the military draft, and settling on a career.

And all of that was held in tension with the family foundations that were laid for me to enter eventually into a traditional, mainstream expression of Christian ministry. It would begin a long and winding journey of self-discovery and spiritual and theological re-orientation. I would seek to learn more about myself, about the "sinful" human condition, about the process of making meaning out of all the disparate sources of information, and about the development of culture and society. I would seek to integrate what we were learning from history, from psychology, and from all the various forms of religion. I would seek to perceive the movement of the divine in the world as best I possibly could, and have it shape how I chose to live.

In a very real sense, I was being "refracted" by that experience. The word describes the change in the direction of a wave of light as it moves from one medium to another, or to the bending of light (or the separation of its elements) as it passes through a prism. We're all familiar with how white light gets refracted into its many colors. In quantum physics, the term "refraction" alludes to how light waves can become particles and to how the creation of new particles actually happens, and how energy gets generated and then experienced. It is an endlessly fascinating topic. For our purposes, I use it to refer to how I have been, and still am, being remade, how meaning was created through the constant process of thoughts and ideas breaking down, only to be replaced by new ones, and then how those thoughts and ideas and perspectives and perceptions evolved and got refined yet again. As we move from one experience to another, and from one way of understanding things to another, it is helpful to think of ourselves as being refracted, as experiencing the creative movement of internal and external forces giving rise to new and more meaningful ways of being, how that which is beyond us and within us continues to transform us to prompt our processes of becoming.

In the chapters to come, I will explore that process of gaining insight and understanding, of growing through painful things and learning how to discover what brings purpose and contentment, of *expanding* our consciousness. I will reference the wonder of human evolution, how cultures developed, and how they can both encourage progress and preclude it. I will reflect on key psychological and emotional concepts, and on how crucial they are to self-understanding and happiness and the work of justice. And I will ponder how current scientific exploration and thought is inextricably linked to our spirituality, our trust, and our ways of being in the world.

Today, I am a teacher and reflector and life-coach. I started out as a student of theology and psychology, becoming a parish minister in the moderate and mainstream Lutheran Church (ELCA) in the upper mid-west. As I deepened my learning and understanding, I transitioned to a career as a hospital chaplain, and then to becoming a bioethicist and a teacher of pan-religious clinical ministry in major medical centers, the modern temples of American medicine and culture. Throughout my personal and professional journey, I was drawn not only to the drama of life and death experiences, but to the writings of key researchers, progressive thinkers, astute social analyzers, and the "wise ones" of the spiritual and religious traditions. It all made for a wonderful "unfolding" into expanding my insight and toward learning how to live a fulfilling and meaningful life. I will take the reader through the key concepts, inviting ongoing reflection and integration of new learning at each step.

As I face now my years of slow decline and eventual death, I feel a deep sense of gratitude and equanimity, profoundly appreciative for how I have been . . . what? Shall we say, "cared for?" "Loved?" "Brought along?" Yes, all of those. And I have moved well beyond my original beliefs. Perhaps it is best to say I have come to trust the process and the mysteries and the grace of it all. My soul is mostly at ease. And I am glad for the opportunity to share my reflections.

I had the privilege of spending most of my career caring for ill and dying patients in hospitals and, in a parallel process, of teaching students in ministry in those same hospitals how to provide meaningful and effective spiritual care to every such patient they encountered as chaplains. Many of the patients came into the hospital distressed and anxious about their unfolding illnesses, often in physical crises that gave rise to emotional challenges and struggles of the spirit. In a similar way, many of the students who came into our programs, in turn, were young seminarians on the front end of their spiritual formation. They were largely anxious as well, but also curious and wide open to new learning. And then, like many of the patients who were well into the progression of their illnesses and had already developed significant life experience and wisdom, I was also privileged to work with students who were advanced in their professional development and experienced in ministry. Many of those students, however, were also caught up in inner spiritual conflicts and were struggling to reconcile the teachings of their religious traditions with their own evolving world views. As a result, many of them came into our program to recover from difficult experiences in their congregations, desiring to redirect their vocations. The hospital was a rich environment for learning and growing, for reflection and healing, for deepening perspectives and re-examining previous assumptions, for moving toward greater integration of self-understanding and the tenets of faith, and for profound personal growth for both patients and clinical practitioners.

The first time I walked into a patient's room (I was 24 and very raw) my academic knowledge and minimal clinical training deserted me. I felt terribly ill-equipped and inadequate. But I was lucky. Beth was an older white woman, from my same religious and ethnic tradition, and she took good care of me. She was declining from cancer, and would be unlikely to leave the hospital, according to the nurse. She took my hand, told me how grateful she was that I had come to "visit" her, and told me about her life on the farm and the death of her husband two years prior. She was ready to let go of this life, she said, confident in the one to come, seemingly fully grounded in her Lutheran faith. Then she asked me to read her a Psalm and to say a prayer. And I relaxed as she talked, became able to express my empathy and care, and even able to stand in the intimacy of her openness with her, so reminded was I of my grandmother, a gentle and saintly woman. I had felt anxious entering her room; I felt honored and privileged leaving it, and I had a sense that a new world was opening up for me.

But the next day I was asked by that same nurse to go and see Bryce. She told me that Bryce was 28 years old and a former linebacker for a professional football team. And, that he was dying of metastatic intestinal cancer. I gulped hard. It was one thing to express my care for an elderly and grandmotherly Scandinavian; it was quite another thing to try to connect with a pro athlete, very near to my own age. It instantly raised up all my insecurities; I did not want to knock on that door. But I gathered myself and tentatively proceeded, met by the patient's wife, a stunningly beautiful young woman who had been one of the team's cheerleaders, and my felt inadequacy only increased. Bryce was sleeping, she told me, so I spoke softly and turned to leave. "Stay" came the word from the bed, and I turned back. "But I don't want any bullshit." Okay, I thought, time for some straight conversation. But what really was my purpose in that room? Why did I think I had any agency to speak to this guy? Such questions would shape my inner journey for the next many years. There would be no room for "bullshit," no room for denial, no room for facile explanations or party-line religious reflections based in anything other than grounded facts and reality.

I don't remember what was said at that point, only that I was taken in by this 250-pound rock-hard man. I met his eyes, swallowed hard, pulled up a chair, and he softened immediately. His eyes filled with tears, and he told me his story. He just wanted to talk, and it was clear he just wanted me to listen. I did. And I became aware of the cathartic power of story, of reflection, of exploration. He was afraid of dying, he was angry, and yet he was profoundly gentle. Toward the end, he grabbed my arm and, in an anguished cry that came from his depths, effused "This thing is eating me alive, and I can't do a damn thing about it!" I remember leaving his room that day and slamming my foot into the wall. I didn't know how to process my frustration—my lack of understanding and insight, my spiritual pain—as I took in the harsh realities and began to face more honestly the rampaging mysteries of living and dying. I was learning about the hard realities in a new and profoundly unsettling way. I was confronting my own helplessness, the deep angst of the human condition, the brokenness and uncertainty and fragility of life. It was a lesson I would never forget.

I stayed with Bryce and Connie through the next several days, until he slipped into unconsciousness. I remember securing their room for privacy, telling Connie to crawl into bed with him where they could hold each other, and advocating for his comfort. When he died, I was deeply saddened but I also had a distinct feeling of gratitude. He—they—had taught me so much, and it radically changed my life, from reactor to seeker, from accommodator to engager. It was time to step up and in.

Over the next forty-plus years, my learning would continue, my life would evolve, and my heart would deepen, never easily but always insistently. I would face conflicts, losses, suffering, injustice, misunderstanding and rejection. And I would experience success and growth and love and acceptance and unlimited support from many people. It would become a fascinating and difficult and wonderful and profoundly meaningful journey. My patients taught me all about navigating life in all its complexities and wonders, honestly, straightforwardly, openly. From the first time I held a 23-week fetus in the palm of my hand as I baptized her and as her heart slowed to a stop, to the teenagers who were dying from blood diseases, to the dozens of patients whose lives changed in an instant from active and vital to near-total paralysis, to the mostly gay men dying of AIDS, to the hard-bitten business men dying of heart failure, to those who endured the wrenching wait for a hoped-for heart transplant—some making it, most not—to the ones in unendurable pain whom we helped die, I was shaped, deepened, softened and re-made. I would get to work closely, even intimately, with nurses and physicians, with students of all stripes, with people who were suffering and with people who were in the full flower of becoming. It was a profound privilege to be brought into the intimate spaces of thousands of people, and the fires tempered me and transformed me and renewed me. And, I am so very grateful.

My students taught me as well. As they struggled to make sense out of their own experiences and to integrate their personal and professional self-understanding, I would identify with them, wrestle with them, seek to empower them, re-direct them and challenge them, always inviting them into the process of becoming more than they were before. As I did so, I would be fascinated and grateful, always learning from their courage and wisdom and trust.

I will share what I have learned over these next few chapters. But perhaps more than that, I hope to stimulate the reader to think in new ways, to explore beyond the boundaries of their childhood teachings, to embrace new ways of being and perceiving and living. "God" knows—in these days of social unrest and division and threat—that we all need to open ourselves to new learning and to new ways of being, and to live into new levels of spiritual intelligence and meaning-making.

To navigate the essence of humanity and of the human psyche is no small thing. To take personal responsibility for one's own spiritual intelligence is a huge step forward. It requires a certain humility—as embodied and projected by great teachers down through the centuries—and it requires a certain commitment to getting up to speed on new knowledge, research data, and global conversation. We draw from it all as we seek to learn and understand, to perceive and discern, to integrate thoughts and feelings and perceptions into a unified and awakened consciousness. This book will reference some of the key concepts and tenets of those teachings; of what we've learned, especially in the last fifty years, of psychology and human emotions, of the processes of thinking and the workings of the human brain, of *process theology* and world religions, of quantum physics, of liminal spiritual experiences, of wisdom and self-fulfillment. *Spiritual intelligence* is about learning to live authentically and in attunement to what we as a species have evolved to embody: the divine spirit of love and beauty within and around us, and the meaningful ways of living in harmony with ourselves, each other, and our world that bring fulfillment and joy.

I welcome you to explore and reflect with me. I invite you to investigate your way of being in the world, to take in new information, to listen to the less-spoken and to the *un*spoken, to let go of what hasn't worked and of what doesn't bring you meaning and joy, to try and "make sense" of things, and to open yourself to renewal and divine wisdom. In so doing, I trust it will assist you in working toward greater justice for others and in building a more meaningful life for yourself. Healthy spirituality is not a mystery; it is a continually life-enhancing response to a curious mind and an open heart. I hope you find it compelling and enriching.

Chapter One

Embracing New Perspectives

"We must accept finite disappointment,
but never lose infinite hope."

—MARTIN LUTHER KING, 2/6/1968

AS A SEMINARIAN IN THE EARLY SEVENTIES, I learned to read and translate classical Greek in order to study the Christian scriptures (the New
Testament of the Bible) in their earliest known forms. The primary purpose was to get at the original intent of the original authors and discern if
key words and meanings had been lost or changed along the way. It is fair
to say that it was an overwhelming and fluid challenge, since so much in
the scriptures had been changed over the centuries. Today we have over
sixty different translations, reflecting differing scholarship, different eras in
which the translation was done, and with differing interpretations of literally thousands of words and passages. Just note the differences between
the King James Version of the Bible, utilizing the more formal "thee"s and
"thou"s of Olde English, and the New Revised Standard Version, completed
and popularized in 1989 and following. Additionally, we have several different paraphrased versions of the Bible, that is, versions that took a popular
English translation and paraphrased the contents into current vernacular.
The Living Bible is one such example, popular for its readability, but held in
disregard by academics.

The study of the field of "biblical criticism" was both arduous and
fascinating, and I began to understand how the texts had been redacted

1

(tweaked and changed, with key words being subtracted or added) along the way. Until the printing press was invented in the mid-1400s, everything in the Bible had been hand copied, over and over again, often by monks who had their own conscious and unconscious biases about the meaning of a particular word or the purpose of a particular text, and then often in ill-lit, drafty rooms. Could it be that mistakes were made . . . that human nature shaped how things got translated . . . that in fact, *purposeful* changes were made? As a still naïve student, I wondered how the scriptures could be divinely *inspired*, if such was the case. Was the Bible really the word of God? And, of course, this question: who were the original authors and what was their real intent?

One beautiful spring day in 1974 I was sitting in class, and we were studying the gospel of Matthew. I had done my homework, carefully translating the assigned pericope (generally a few verses telling of a particular teaching or story). My professor asked me to translate aloud. When I was finished, he disdainfully stated that I had distorted the text by translating the intent of a particular phrase in a broader way than the author had intended. I was confident in my translation and told him so. He responded poorly, taking umbrage, and went on a bit of a rant, ending by claiming that "the gospel of Matthew had lain dormant until (he) finally arrived at the correct translation," seemingly discounting all the academic work of countless scholars that had gone before. Once I got past my initial feelings, I reflected with chagrin on his arrogance and absolute certainty. From that point forward, I held the scriptures gently in my hands, reverently, with a deep appreciation for their *un*-certainty and with a commitment to always approach them contextually, to seek their evolving meaning and figure out how to draw from them in ways that would enhance life for myself and others, and to never to use them as proof-texts, that is as ways to prove a point or an opinion, as if only I had the truth. It was clear to me that they were sacred, that is, that they were deep truths about the human condition and about how to live a meaningful and fulfilling life. What was not clear was whether they were saying deep truths about the divine spirit. Did what was written at that particular time in history reflect the guidance needed to live faithfully today? And what, exactly, did that mean?

I began to understand that ministry—and the study of sacred texts—was a very human endeavor, no different from other service or academic professions, subject to all sorts of human foibles and distortions. During my third year of seminary, I interned at a local hospital and in an alcoholic treatment center. It was a wonderful experience for the most part, except for the fact that my supervisor was himself a closet alcoholic and, though brilliant, was emotionally abusive. I did not realize either of those things at the time; I just suffered the diminishment and abuse as a normal part of the training. Once I got perspective with the help of a good therapist, I understood still further that shadow side of religious teaching and practice, and the slow slide into dysfunction of so many of my teachers and clinical instructors. It was humbling and eye opening at the same time. So many were wonderful role models and kind and compassionate people; but so many were also painfully unintegrated, at risk of acting-out behaviors, and spiritually bereft.

And what I learned was significantly different from what I had come to believe as a child raised in a church-centered family. Since my context was Lutheran Christian, I will focus here on the Christian scriptures and the story of Jesus, though it is a struggle in all major religions. It was an unquestioned given in my culture that the stories in the gospels were historically accurate, and that the letters of Paul were prescriptive for faithful living. We—the "faithful"—took the scriptures *literally*, that is, as grounded in what we believed actually happened two thousand years ago.

I remember coming home from college that first time, after having my eyes opened in my freshman religion class. I told my mother about the long history of creation stories in all the various ancient cultures, and of how the ones in the book of Genesis in the Bible were written as poetry and myth, not as actual history, and that they reflected centuries of evolving perceptions. I had already known that inherently, having been a student of the eras when dinosaurs walked the earth, and had actually found my class liberating and confirming. Not so my mom. Her difficulty in accepting what I was telling her, accompanied by her agitation, sensitized me to both the depth of her beliefs (and the beliefs of so many in my community) and to the challenge of opening them up to a much richer and more beautiful understanding and appreciation. I loved the scriptural stories, all the more so as I came to understand what they symbolically represented, and how they portrayed and represented the efforts of humankind to find spiritual meaning in often very tenuous and oppressed lives. But why had we not been taught the truth of how and why they were written? Literalism just didn't seem to serve my spiritual hunger at all.

Such literalism actually became the policy in the conservative evangelical protestant churches over time, captured in 1978 in their official doctrine of inerrancy, meaning that the Bible is "without error or fault in all its teaching" and is to be understood as the "inspired Word of God." Such absolutism has deeply affected the church and culture, causing all sorts of arguments, rifts, and schisms, most recently seen in the growing and painful political and cultural split in our society at large. We now struggle more than ever with the reality of the conservative political "right" seemingly aligning with the fundamental beliefs of the churches embracing inerrancy, and with the "left" more aligned with a progressive view of the scriptures (meaning open to interpretation) or with Buddhist or Taoist spiritual perspectives, or with no religious beliefs whatsoever. The same struggle pervades the Roman Catholic Church as well, which chronically wrestles internally with issues of autonomy and authority and obedience.

Curiously, it is something of a modern phenomenon. Most historians would note that biblical literalism is really an early 18th century aberration, first taking hold among the Puritan movement in England and then represented by Jonathan Edwards, among others, in the United States. It was Edwards who preached against rationalism and skepticism and promoted concepts of conversion and revivalism, becoming the progenitor of today's evangelical right. Prior to that the scriptures were generally embraced as necessary for faith and life and "salvation," but more as guidelines and sources of wisdom and inspiration than as absolute requirements.

I was thirteen years old when I was invited by a friend's family to go with them to hear Billy Graham, who was having a "crusade" at the Minnesota State Fairgrounds. Graham was a literalist, and he had become something of a celebrity in the news and on TV, preaching in England at the Queen's request and meeting with presidents and other world leaders. But I was reluctant to go, being aware of my friend's evangelical bent. His father was a prominent Lutheran minister who didn't fit the mold of being stoic and self-contained. Nonetheless, I joined them, somewhat tenuously. Graham presented an impressive figure, tall and handsome, and he was a forceful and captivating speaker. I was aware that my friend's family appeared mesmerized. Graham's process was to make we listeners fully aware of our sinful natures, invite silent confession and a desire to live a moral and faithful life, and then publicly "accept" Jesus as "personal lord and savior"—indeed, to be "born again." It meant responding to his invitation to walk down in front of the altar and meet with a "counselor" to make both confession and profession. Well, in my very tentative way, I realized I just didn't trust what I was seeing and hearing. And I didn't like the emotional appeal and the requirement to somehow give myself over to something I didn't fully understand. As a matter of fact, I remember feeling mildly irritated, as if the expectation was that I comply with an external authority to something that was deeply personal and, to that point, very private. Weren't matters of faith *supposed* to be private? Matters of spirituality were already causing consternation for me, just as I was entering my teenage years. I resisted the invitation to go to the altar, even though my friend's whole family did so. My spiritual intelligence was beginning to grow, characterized—as it would so often be—by a touch of defiance and no little self-doubt. But my course was being set, and for the next many years I would ponder and study the nature of faith in God, and attempt to discern the key messages to enhance the meaning of my life.

It was Martin Luther King Jr. who opened the door for deeper learning in me. That same year, still thirteen years old, I was taken in by his moving *I Have A Dream* speech given on the Lincoln Memorial steps following the March on Washington in 1963. It was a prophetic and peaceful demonstration calling for civil rights and freedom from the pervasive racism in our country, most especially in the South where it was openly expressed. As King got into his speech, he set aside his notes, with the poetic and powerful words flowing out of him, words rooted in the Christian gospel, words that both convicted those who perpetuated the horrors of two centuries of slavery and abuse, and words that gave people of all races and circumstances a profoundly hopeful vision. I was only vaguely aware that he was putting his life in danger, that he was willing to call out the racism of white supremacists and motivate others, both black and white, to work for greater justice and equality, while exposing himself to great risk. What a time it was! Who can forget the abuse thrown at the African American college students during the sit-in at the Woolworth's lunch counter in Greensboro, North Carolina, or the water cannons and dogs of Bull Connor, the Commissioner of Public Safety in Birmingham, Alabama, who used them indiscriminately against the civil rights advocates of the Southern Christian Leadership Conference that same year? Or the lynchings or the murders or the cross burnings of the Ku Klux Klan? For this early adolescent, it was a time of *becoming*, trying to take in the meaning of it all, trying to understand, trying to figure out what it would mean for me as I grew into an adult.

That the evangelical white church in America today should passively align itself with the structures that maintain the racial divide reveals the underlying distortions of a dualistic theology and a spiritually vulnerable faith. Note today the false righteousness of targeting and condemning academic perspectives, such as Critical Race Theory. And note the irony of how unconscious racism has become so deeply embedded in our institutions that no less a bright light than Cornel West would choose to resign from the faculty of Harvard Theological School. Such painful realities reflect distorted and dysfunctional expressions of religiosity, and fail to reflect any meaningful spirituality.

Spirituality is that human quality that recognizes the divine in the other, that honors and respects all of life, that treats all people with reverence and compassion and love. To do otherwise is to self-limit and isolate, and thus we see the retrenchment of those who seek to control and maintain the status quo. The word spirituality, by nature of its Greek roots, points to a dynamic, ever-flowing movement of divine energy. Seeking to maintain the status quo is antithetical to the meaning of the word.

It is notable that the citizens of the state of Georgia elected Rev. Raphael Warnock to serve as a senator from the state of Georgia. He was and still is serving as the Senior Pastor at Ebenezer Baptist Church in Atlanta, the same church where Martin Luther King served. The Black Church is distinct today in the South, advancing a culture of prophetic engagement and servanthood, far from the dominant culture of white conservatives. That Warnock should win the state-wide election in Georgia is truly historic, not just for electing that state's first black senator, but because of the promotion of significant spiritual truths. Warnock seems to have integrated his spiritual understanding profoundly well, speaking in gentle and loving terms about painful and difficult realities, always focusing on justice, compassion, and prophetic engagement. He notes that his political life is consistent with his ministry, based on the biblical concept of servanthood. The contrast to white evangelical literalism and its tacit acceptance of racism cannot be greater. It bodes, perhaps, a new day on the political landscape, and serves as reminder of the power of spiritual grounding.

I note also the profound impact of Amanda Gorman, the twenty-two year old black woman, recently named the National Youth Poet Laureate, who spoke at President Biden's Inauguration Ceremony. So spiritually intelligent and attuned was she, that she put her finger on the ethos of the entire nation. Her presence, her grace, her prophetic voice—her spirituality—served to inspire and uplift in ways no one else could match on that momentous day. Gorman and Warnock follow well in the footsteps of, and stand strong on the shoulders of, their predecessors: Howard Thurman, Maya Angelou, Audre Lorde, W.E.B. Du Bois, Toni Morrison, and of course, Martin Luther King.

So significant was King to me that when I went into the seminary as a twenty-two year old, confused and anxious, especially about preaching, I found a vinyl record album of King's most revered sermons, recorded live as he gave them. I wore that record out, listening to it over and over again, practicing his delivery and his cadence in front of the mirror and learning how to emphasize key words and phrases. It is something of a humorous and incongruous picture of a young white boy in Minnesota trying to emulate the voice of the greatest Black preacher and movement leader in our country's history. But nonetheless, it shaped my mind and touched my soul in ways I did not previously understand. And perhaps more than anything, as I *listened* to his words and to his message, I tried to take in his theology and his convictions and his hope and his courage.

Far more than the "fathers" of my own Anglo-European Lutheran tradition, from the original Martin Luther on down, it was King who shaped my thinking and empowered my voice. Martin Luther King Jr. was not a literalist. Being a biblical scholar, he set things in context, and always spoke about how the ancient texts could be seen to speak to this time and to these events. He portrayed the Jesus of the gospels as one who always worked for justice and equality, as a healer, not just of those sick in body, but of those sick in their souls, of whole classes of people and whole communities. He never spoke in hostility toward those who persecuted him and jailed him and ridiculed him; he always conveyed his compassion for the inner prisons in which they were caught, and which was of their own making. He was a remarkable witness. And his ministry exposed both the rigid literalism inherent in the racist white culture of the South and the fear of those who were willing to venture out into a new and more inclusive way of being. We are left today with more of the same. Historians and sociologists note the truth of King's reflection that the arc of the moral universe is indeed long, only slowly "bending toward justice." We have come a long way in these past sixty years, yet even now we have white power brokers attempting to preserve a racist system, a false faith, and a morally corrupt social structure. It is true—to paraphrase the great Irish biblical scholar John Dominic Crossan—that the scriptures never say *I reject your justice because of your lack of worship*, but rather, that they repeatedly convey the thought of *I reject your worship because of your lack of justice*.

The murmurings have been present for a long time. During the 70s and 80s there was a significant emphasis in the Christian Church, and particularly in the Catholic Church, on what was called "charismatic renewal." It tended to reflect a somewhat fragmented focus on a particular image of what has been traditionally called the "Holy Spirit" and on what was referenced in Paul's writings as "the *gifts* of the spirit." Those churches that embraced that emphasis were, in fact, onto something, calling out the dominant culture of the church as spiritually tepid and lacking the key components of vitality and social engagement. However, it grabbed the attention of the media by advancing such fringe concepts as speaking in tongues and physical healings, and gave rise to a few questionable media stars, the forerunners of today's mega-church pastors. It seemed primarily to take hold in fundamentalist churches, and with a core group of conservative Catholics, and on the fringes of more mainstream denominations.

During the spring of my final year at the seminary as I was preparing to take a parish position, the pastor of my home congregation in St. Paul told me that his brother's church, in a small northern Minnesota town, needed a new associate pastor. Might I be interested? I knew that pastor was somewhat "charismatic", but I needed a job, and the interview was arranged. And I loved the north woods and lakes. The interview itself went well; the people of the church "council" were kind and interested and affirming, and my anxiety slowly faded as my confidence grew. And they were curious about what I would bring, seemingly interested in my emphasis on what was then called the "social gospel" with its focus on peacemaking and justice. But following the interview, as we were having the traditional coffee and Scandinavian cookies and just chatting, the pastor came up to me, congratulated me on doing well, and then, with his council president, told me out of the blue that we would next go back to the parsonage where they would "lay their hands" on me and give me the gifts of the spirit. I was taken aback, to say the least. I scrambled to think how to respond, feeling like I was right back at that Billy Graham crusade once again. Finally, I gently said I didn't think that would be appropriate, and that we needed to get to know each other better, or something like that. He smiled and leaned over and then whispered to me: "either we do that, and you get the job, or we don't do that, and you don't get the job." I made the long drive home rather shaken, having declined the imperative. I was learning significant things about the church and the real world of professional ministry. And I was filled with significant doubt. "Is this really what I want to do?" I pondered. "Why do people hold such variant views, and why so rigidly?" It was not at all what I had envisioned.

I was becoming progressively aware of wanting to become more spiritually intelligent somehow, more attuned to what the life force of the universe was all about and how it engaged with me personally. As a soon-to-be parish pastor, I was supposed to promote a way of being and a particular belief system that reflected our Lutheran Christian tradition and creedal perspectives. And I was to care for and support the people of my congregation in all matters of faith and life. How could I do that successfully and effectively when I didn't dwell there myself? How could I help others care for their own souls and deepen their spiritual lives when mine was still evolving, and when the split between tentatively progressive thinkers like me and conservative/evangelical/charismatic folks was clearly widening?

Indeed, that gap has only widened further. Today's evangelicals have, unfortunately, strayed far from core spiritual constructs. It has been both disheartening and fascinating to observe the slow distortion of the evangelical church since aligning itself with Donald Trump, Fox News, and right-wing politics, even embracing such conspiracy theories as a fraudulent presidential election. That elected Republican congresspeople and senators and evangelical leaders could remain complicitly silent, while lies were told from the White House and while the Proud Boys and Oath Keepers chanted racist and antisemitic slogans, reveals the profound struggle at the center of the evangelical church.

Sadly today, the spiritual decline appears to be continuing in the evangelical churches aligned with the political far right, with even many congregational pastors and other leaders blindly unself-aware and locked into rigid and exclusive perspectives. Today's "conservative" church seems to have gone the way of white nationalism, authoritarianism, and a sort of post-truth, easy-answer faith where the promise of salvation comes through mindless compliance with the directions of glamorously wealthy celebrity leaders and preachers, and the clear rejection of all things outside the cult. This "new" religion is neither rooted in the Christian gospel nor in academic study nor in personal reflection and integration. It is, sadly, born, like its politics, out of fear and resentment and hopelessness.

Yet, while such "gaslighting" and distortion seems to grab the dominant attention of the media, something else is clearly happening. Not just in the United States, but around the world there is a counter-movement, a growing interest in all things spiritual. New books, new websites, new expressions of hunger for thoughtful, realistic and compassionate frame-works for making meaning in life are proliferating. The scriptures of all religions are being re-studied; poets and musicians and artists and writers are reflecting on our struggles and seeking new ways of being and new ways for coming together. As more and more people are tuning into the negative effects of social division and climate change, spiritual intelligence, now grounded in academic, scientific and professional research, is rising. Though these are challenging days in so many ways, so are they hopeful and exciting. It is a time of change, a time for reflection, and a time of hope.

Chapter Two

Coming of Age

"If you don't know where you are going, any road will get you there."

—LEWIS CARROLL, *ALICE IN WONDERLAND*

"It's not what happens to you, but how you react to it that matters."

—EPICTETUS, *THE ENCHIRIDION*

BECOMING MORE SPIRITUALLY INTELLIGENT entails working to discover the truth about—and make sense of—the things that we have previously accepted without understanding or even questioning their nature. The scriptures are full of such stories, stories that we only slowly recast from supposed historical events to profound literary devices meant to metaphorically describe significant human experiences. Both the Hebrew and the Christian scriptures are filled with them, beautiful stories of coming to awareness, of recognition of place and creatureliness, of growing into self-awareness, of repentance and realignment. There are empowering scriptural stories, motivating stories, humbling stories. There are stories that elucidate our struggles and insights, and stories that obfuscate; stories that expose our shortcomings and stories that generate hope and courage. There are stories of spiritual liberation, of emotional imprisonment, of the timeless effort to work for justice and ensure the greater good for the greater number. And there are countless stories of coming to self-awareness, and of evolving moral perspectives, and of struggling to become whatever it means to be fully human.

All the stories reflect "truth" per se, though many, if not most, of them are something less than historical accounts. The Bible is a collection of some of the most meaningful and enduring stories of human history. Taken together, they have shaped the thinking and behavior and beliefs of countless people since the canon was set back in the fourth century. We have reflected on them, parsed them, argued them, promoted them, preached on them and drawn from them for inspiration, comfort, guidance and understanding. Such stories have become a way of passing on time-less lessons, of perpetuating cultural norms, of teaching and of capturing our imaginations, of motivating us and encouraging us. They capture our never-ending struggle to perceive the unfolding meaning of life and to face our life passages and frailties and death. They elucidate and they cloud, they convict and lift up, they generate pain and joy as well as tears and hope. I am so grateful for the stories I was given as a child, the family stories and the funny stories and the off-color ones and the ones about wisdom and courage. I am grateful for the books that were read to me, for the countless times I sat in church listening to the Bible stories, for the inspiring stories I would read in the magazines or in the library. I came to love sitting quietly, listening to my relatives, or soaking up the silence in the beautiful Carnegie library just a block from home, perusing whatever caught my interest.

Indeed, spiritual intelligence is a reflection of living *into* the stories, of deciphering their meaning, and of creating new meaning. We read to have our consciousness expanded, to learn, to better understand things, whether it be the Bible, the New York Times, an autobiography or a good novel. We seek to be engaged, and to discern, and to integrate new thoughts and ways of being. We read to *enhance* our lives. Ought preaching and teaching and worship experiences not do the same? The Spirit seems to always be calling us forward, into deeper consideration, into exploration, into trans-formative ways of being. We read to learn, and we *learn* to enhance our lives and to respond to the embedded but unspoken invitation to assent to newness. Such is the process of thinking and re-creating our lives. Religious faith ought never be about following blindly, or about obedience or worse, compliance. It is always about transformation and becoming someone new.

Coming of Age

As an adult, I have come to love sitting in older, traditional churches, looking, listening, reflecting, and just being still, allowing my mind to open and wander. They have become places of solitude and solace for me, filled with the imprint of the millions of seekers and pilgrims and priests and contributors who proceeded me. I am often profoundly moved, renewed somehow in my soul. My favorite places in the world are the cathedrals of Europe, among them Chartres in France, St. Stephen's in Vienna, St. Vitus's in Prague, and Canterbury, York, Salisbury and so many others in England, Scotland and Ireland. They have been liminal places for me, where the veil between the physical and spiritual is somehow thinned out, where the divine presence is felt and experienced in new ways. I have loved walking and pausing reverently though them, and not only the churches but through the many old monastery ruins and stone circles and henges, scattered throughout the British Isles and Europe. I love to think about who had gone there before, and how I was now joining with them, inviting them to speak to me and guide me and renew me. While in Glastonbury, I momentarily felt surrounded and nurtured by those who had worshipped there centuries before. In a monastery ruin just outside Llangolen, Wales, I had the sense that I was actually hearing the monks singing a Gregorian chant as I stood where the choir had once been, and my soul was uplifted. At Whitby Abbey in North Yorkshire, it seemed as though I could momentarily glimpse the long-gone high altar in front of the now-vacant triptych windows, and I could sense the gentle and compassionate energy flowing through the sanctuary.

My affinity for such places no doubt was born by attending services as a child in my home congregation. I would often sit with my grandparents, (when my parents were otherwise occupied ushering and in the choir) who nurtured me with unconditional love. I loved the stories, and I loved the silence, and I loved the singing of the beautiful hymns, and the sense of uplift when the pastor would pronounce words of forgiveness and reconciliation, and the intimacy of walking forward to the altar to receive communion. The yearly highlight for me always was staying up late to go to the 11:00 candlelight service on Christmas Eve, during our cold and dark Minnesota Decembers, to hear the *story* of Jesus' birth, and to join in the singing of *Silent Night* and *Angels We Have Heard On High* and *O, Little Town of Bethlehem*. During such moments, I felt connected to something beyond myself, loved, accepted, a bit awed, at peace. Later, when I was a parish pastor myself, those were the things that kept me in it for eight years. I loved the passing on of the stories, the preaching and the worship and the singing of the old familiar hymns most of all.

But also, as a child, my questioning mind tended to be tempered by my Sunday School teachers and later by my confirmation teachers. The fallback position of most of them, including my mom, was to just "accept things by faith" which, of course, directly led to my questioning of the tenets of our faith, and to my curiosity to continue to learn about and explore what they meant by *faith* and *spirituality*. I often pushed back; I occasionally rebelled. Yet I loved much of what I experienced in my church congregation which, after all, was just three houses down from where we lived. The women of the congregation, especially, were kind and nurturing. So, I joined the kids' choirs and the Cub Scouts and eventually became the Luther League (the high school youth group) president, and helped to organize our activities. I liked to pull together discussion groups on current topics and fun activities like softball and ski trips and lock-ins where we would play games and flirt all night, but mostly I had the sense that an opportunity was being placed before me. It was a bit confusing. Perhaps I was being "called" into ministry, but what the heck did that actually mean?

I became significantly invested in the life of the church but profoundly ambivalent about it at the same time. Even as I loved the tradition and the rituals and the music, I was learning about what a human institution the church was and about how limited it seemed to be able to bring about social justice, the struggle for which was now dominating the airways. I realize I was probably no different than any of my peers as a teenager in that we found the whole church thing somewhat odd. I was both attracted and repelled, both drawn to the spiritual and turned off by the hierarchy and paternalism. What was I to do with it all?

I had a fairly rosy, if naïve, view of life then, and was doing mostly well, from a teenage *angst* perspective, being pretty much on track in my development. I was socially extroverted, a good student, and I made friends easily, for the most part. But then in the spring of that profoundly painful year of 1968, my high school graduation just two months away, we held a youth-led Sunday service. It occurred just after Martin Luther King was murdered and just before Robert Kennedy was killed. I had some things I wanted to say about social justice and civil rights and peacemaking, so I agreed to be one of the speakers, though my bravado was compromised by my self-consciousness, and I was nervous and halting. My friend, Bob, who had a rock 'n roll band, agreed to play, and the band set up in the choir

loft, doing a rock version of the Lord's Prayer and a couple other question-
ably prophetic folk-rock songs. It was a momentous day, clearly pushing
the envelope in that staid congregation. Our church sat at the foot of the
largest Lutheran Seminary in the country, and many of the professors were
members of the congregation.

It was one of them, an old-school prof who had emigrated from eastern Europe, who came up to me after the service, somewhat florid and
breathless, and said "You will go to hell!" and then turned and walked away.
Phew! It was my first formal introduction to the dysfunction of religious
life and its endemic intolerance of difference and change. Even as I appreciated his own history that may have led him to say such a thing to me, I
found it deeply distressing. I remember my folks didn't say anything at all to
me afterwards, a painfully critical silence. I suspect they were embarrassed,
perhaps even ashamed. And I buried the hurt, and became, if anything, less
trusting and accepting, a bit more defiant and, frankly, somewhat lost. It
would prove to be a turning point.

To that moment, my journey through growing up, if periodically
painful, had been mostly pretty gentle; I was one of the lucky ones, surrounded by a stable home, good friends and teachers and resources, and a
mostly helpful church community, all of which undergirded my desire to
learn. I didn't "act out" much as a teenager. Friends of mine, whose parents
were abusive or struggled with alcohol abuse, or who themselves had been
abused and were now parenting out of disordered personalities, tended to
seek out higher highs, while also tending to experience lower lows. But with
nurturing relatives and a questioning mind, my learning and development
kept moving forward.

And I was supported unconditionally by one close friend. I had no
clue at the time that Jeffrey was struggling with his identity and his sexual
preference, but I loved his reflective and sensitive way of being, his gently
humorous self-deprecation, his wry wisdom. He was such a gift to me. Jeffrey eventually came out in his early twenties, but during our adolescence
he was the kind and empathic and warmly accepting friend I needed to
just help get me through. I was a true child of the 60s, a child of rock 'n
roll, of the struggle for civil rights, of social upheaval and rapid change. I
found it stimulating, troubling, challenging, and yet full of hope. My parents and community, however, tended to want to tamp down the chaos and
the enthusiasm and protect the status quo, naturally. And so, where I saw
myself as an extrovert seeking new experiences and understanding, I was

pretty much labeled the non-compliant one and the rebel in my family, a dichotomy I would find difficult for years. I realized I was a bit of a fish out of water, and therefore realized that I was pretty much on my own, with my other two siblings being five and seven years older. The next several years would prove difficult and somewhat lonely, and there was nothing for it but to learn.

I was only eleven years old when I began to awaken to the realities of the outside world. It was the civil rights struggle, presented by Walter Cronkite every evening at 5:30, that most prominently broke into my consciousness, with the Freedom Riders' efforts to challenge the segregation laws in the South in '61 and '62, with the violence surrounding the effort to guarantee voting rights, with MLK's speech in '63, all followed by the assassination of JFK in November of that year. I consider '63 my year of coming into consciousness, when I began seeing the inherent difficulties embedded in the human community, when I began to open up and wise up. I was beginning to see the oppression of people of color in our society, and the poverty and classism, and the discrimination of most anyone who didn't fit the dominant white upper middle class culture. And then I went to church with my father on that horrible evening of November 22nd, just hours after Kennedy had been shot in Dallas. I remember wondering why no one was speaking to my shock and horror and confusion. My father didn't say a word, but I could see that he was distressed. I just didn't know what it meant, since we were a culturally stoic family and didn't talk about feelings. The more social unrest, the greater the silence.

And then the flood gates opened as I entered high school. The British Invasion, the Viet Nam War, Kent State, the Summer of Love, Hendrix and Joplin and the Airplane, and the assassinations in the Spring of '68. Later would come Woodstock and the draft. But during that summer after my high school graduation, we all tuned in to the Democratic National Convention in Chicago. Hubert Humphrey, our senator, was likely to be nominated as a candidate for President, and all the journalists wrote about how the social unrest over the Viet Nam war was turning Chicago into a powder keg. Getting ready to go off to college, I read everything I could about the Youth International Party (Abbie Hoffman and Jerry Rubin) and the Students for a Democratic Society (Tom Hayden and Rennie Davis). And I watched with fascination as Chicago erupted in protests and police violence. The trial of the Chicago 7 and of Bobby Seale (of the Black Panthers) followed, dominating the news, and our family struggled. My brother was in the Navy and overseas, my folks found the protest movement abhorrent, and I was thinking, even then, that the repression by Mayor Daley's city government and the Chicago police was completely antithetical to what were becoming my somehow-poorly-regarded "liberal" values. It was exciting, troubling and isolating all at the same time. It might be said that it was the best of times and the worst of times. And it was all amazing and unsettling and even somewhat frightening. And lonely. And the pre-eminent question in front of me, as it was for so many of my peers, was "how, then, shall I then live?" It was a question posed repeatedly in the scriptures and then re-formulated by the ethicist H. Richard Niebuhr during World War II, who along with his brother, the great social commentator and theologian Reinhold Niebuhr, would greatly influence my thought process for years to come. I took the question to heart: what did it mean, what *would* it mean, to live a truly moral life?

A bit more context: my mother's father (the retired Lutheran pastor) was something of a benevolent patriarch. My seven uncles were towering figures to me, all successful and a bit rakish, and I loved the gatherings with all my cousins at my grandparents' every summer. My dad was an engineer in the Minnesota Highway Department, also born of second-generation immigrant Scandinavian parents, and he was both hard-working and emotionally remote. Mom was dutiful, gentle, and assumed her traditional female roles without complaint. My sister, the first born, had lots of friends and was a good student whose world was foreign to me, and my brother reflected my father to a tee. As the trailing child, I was both afforded freedom and largely ignored. For the most part, I did just fine. But I was also insecure and struggled with my self-esteem. And I was mildly repressed, tentative, and a bit resentful. I wanted more, somehow. I wanted to be engaged and relevant and feel like I had a purpose. And I sure didn't like the feeling of being the least important.

Following that awful experience of youth Sunday, when my illusions about ministry got confronted and when I was set somewhat apart from my family, and when I found myself feeling isolated and tentative, I might have reoriented and gone after a secular career in the social sciences. Instead, I both gave a tentative affirmative response to my inner stirrings and I "gave in" to parental expectations. Still being caught in the web of my family's unconscious script, I agreed to go to the Lutheran college that my mother had attended, in part to please her, but also in part because it was 250 miles away from home, which was what really mattered to me. I wanted to explore my freedom, not unlike most of my peers. And I talked a good buddy into going with me and being roommates, the final motivation. And I wanted to figure things out, but my struggle with anxiety and confusion became if anything, more acute. My ambivalence about the future, and about who I was and how I might best live, deepened. My childhood faith was hanging on by a thread. And the pull toward getting out on the street with the protesters came hard up against the small private college's conservative culture. I felt torn. I was not living the life I wanted; I was not being who I wanted to be, even as I was able to make friends and get into the academics. As a result, I experienced significant discouragement during the first two years of college, feeling spiritually bereft and acting out in ways I didn't like and which made me feel less than okay, and I was unclear about how to proceed or what field of study to make my major. I realized a needed to make a change.

However, two classes during my freshman year began to stir my heart and turn me toward a new way of being. The first was a Sociology of Religion class, focused on how humankind first began to think about creation and the divine, and how such concepts evolved over the centuries. We learned how the scriptures came to be written, and what the intent was of the original authors. We were taught very clearly about the dangers of literalism and the challenge of getting beneath the text to the deeper and often subtle meaning. The other one was my Introduction to Psychology class. For the first time, my feelings and intuition got validated and I began to see how unconscious drives and emotions and thoughts and perceptions shaped our expressions more than we could ever be aware. Two new pathways opened up, and I pursued both of them, always seeking the crossroads of religion and psychology, of spirituality and the interplay of the divine with consciousness, of theology and history and sociology.

I transferred to the University of Minnesota in Minneapolis for my junior year to focus on my psychology major, and I immediately got involved in the protest movement. I also faced the lottery for the military draft, and the very real possibility that I could be drafted and sent to fight in Viet Nam. My religious perspectives, my developing values and sense of morality, my concern to act "rightly" and faithfully, all came into play. After talking with my friend Harlan, and then with many people both at the University and in my family and church, and being deeply influenced by what I was reading and seeing and coming to understand, I filed to become a conscientious objector to the draft that was feeding what I considered to be the immoral war effort. I was influenced by the just war theory, by William Sloane Coffin and the Berrigan brothers, by the Niebuhrs, by thoughtful people on both the right and the left and, perhaps most of all, as noted above, by the writings of Martin Luther King, the devout and brilliant Christian minister and now social prophet and moral figurehead. More than anything, I wanted to reflect the same core convictions about which he wrote. It was both a painful and powerful time, a challenging and deeply inspiring learning experience. I learned about my bottom-line values, I discovered internal strength and resolve. But I also felt isolated and anxious. And I learned more about my family, both good and awful. I could sense a rising up of spirit within me, a growing sense of self, a desire to become something more. How then, should I live?

It all came to a head one evening at the supper table with my parents and grandfather. I was living at home for that school year and, with my grandmother in a care center, my maternal grandfather was living at home with us as well, now 92 years old. I had spoken with him at length over the previous couple of years, exploring issues of faith and life and seeking his wisdom and my deeper understanding, and he had a wonderful and profound perspective on what he always referred to as the "Christian gospel" and its foundation of justice and love. I realize now that it must have been hard for my father to see that I had developed a closer relationship with my grandfather than with him. And it must have been harder still to have my grandfather move into the house with us. Indeed, I later learned how difficult that relationship had occasionally been, and how frustrated and resentful my father sometimes felt. Add to it the powerlessness he experienced as a result of my resistance to his guidance and his deep dismay about my decision to become a conscientious objector to the draft, and the situation was ripe for a blow-up.

My father initiated the conversation at supper one evening by asking if I had settled on a major field of study yet, clearly intending to steer me toward engineering like my brother. When I stated that I had settled on psychology, he blurted something about it being a "quack" profession, revealing both his disappointment and how narrow his world view had become. Silence ensued for the next half minute or so. And then, in a rare outburst, he pounded his hands on the table, got up and stomped out of the house, slamming the front door as he left. My mom was shaken. She got up mid-meal as well, cleared the table, and just stood at the kitchen sink, quietly crying. True to form, not a word was said. And I felt paralyzed, near tears myself.

Such are the experiences that can profoundly impact our psyches and shape our future ways of being. Had it been left there, I suspect it would have led to long-term alienation. I withdrew to my room until, an hour or so later, my grandfather called up and asked if I would come back downstairs. My father had returned, and my grandfather had requested a family meeting to sort things out. He asked my parents to sit together on the couch, and placed me in the big chair to the right. And then he got up in front of us all, supporting himself with his cane, an Abrahamic figure, and talked about his sorrow at what had happened and about his love for us all. Being a former pastor, he referenced appropriate scriptures and reflected, with a tremor in his voice and fire in his eyes, about what those writings meant for our lives and our relationships. And they were things I had never heard put in that same way in all the countless church services I had attended. I was mesmerized. The words that changed my life that night then came at the end. He moved over and stood right next to me, putting his hand on my shoulder. And then he said to my parents, "This is my grandson whom I love. And I will support him, whatever he chooses to do with his life." And then he leaned in toward my parents: "And so will you!" he said. And so will you.

I learned a lot that night. I became aware that I didn't ever want to go through something like that again. I became aware of my father's limitations and frustrations, even as I recognized his desire to connect with me. I became much clearer about my own vocational direction and about how I wanted to be experienced by others. Years later, I would refer to that event as "my calling into ministry." I wanted to learn to be able to do for others what my grandfather had done for me. It was an experience of unconditional positive regard, of profound acceptance and respect and support. And from it, I learned in a new way that I was "okay" at my core. My grandfather's intervention shifted my emotional state and embedded a new spiritual reality—to stand up, to speak truth, to seek authentic expressions of love. It was a powerful experience that deepened and softened me as a human being, that began to open me up, that fed my soul. My journey from that point on would be two steps forward, one step back, sometimes following the right path, sometimes the wrong one, occasionally acting in ways that went against my own intent and being self-limiting and hurtful toward others more often than I would like to admit, but experience is a wonderful teacher, even when painful. And I am grateful for the learning. It set my course and, though difficult, it helped me reflect on who I wanted to become. I was beginning to understand what it meant to be a spiritually-alive person and it would become a life quest to continue to refine it.

Chapter Three

Humanity and Divinity

"Science can purify religion from error and superstition. Religion can purify science from idolatry and false absolutes. Each can draw the other into a wider world, a world in which both can flourish."

—POPE JOHN PAUL II, *PAPAL LETTER*

"I have set before you this day life and death, good and evil, blessing and curse. Therefore, choose life."

—MOSES, *DEUTERONOMY* 30:19

I NO LONGER SUBSCRIBE to a particular theological perspective or creedal confession. My image of the divine, my spiritual practices, my perspectives on Christianity—indeed, my perspectives on all other religious formulations—have all evolved and deepened. As they did so, I slowly experienced what I can only describe as a kind of broadening, an opening up, a coming alive. It can be said that learning to let go of the traditions that I had been taught in my early life saved my faith, though today it is a faith that is founded on the embrace of mystery and on trust in that which is mostly hidden and undefinable. I tend to describe myself today as *post*-Christian, and as no longer religious, that is, as someone who consciously seeks to transcend human conceptions and images of God that have constrained us from feeling spiritually alive and attuned, but also as one who is profoundly shaped by ongoing engagement from what I now call the divine spirit. My continuing experience has been about becoming progressively "more than" I was previously. As I slowly let go and let myself fall into what I used to describe as the "grace of God," trusting that I was being gently pulled into greater awareness, I discovered that my spirituality continued to expand and grow and my reverence *for*, and my connection *to* the divine spirit, only deepened.

Much of that evolution turned on two things: my study of human history and my study of the scriptures (and particularly on the quest to understand better the story of Jesus). As a Lutheran Christian studying to become a professional pastor, I wanted greater knowledge and understanding in both areas. How did we evolve into self-aware and extremely complex individuals, capable of both great love and great horror? Why do we seem to have both natures? And what role did Jesus and the subsequent church play in the development of, again, both caring communities of faith on the one hand, and hostile and oppressive communities on the other? Who was Jesus really? And what did it mean to "believe" in him? And how did his teachings get so distorted? And how was I to live a life of faith in the face of all the misunderstanding and exclusive thinking and abuses of power? What should that really look like? I loved learning about the brilliant, rebellious, beer-drinking Martin Luther, and about the Reformation that he almost single-handedly put into motion on the European continent, but what was his late-stage antisemitism all about? And was that actually a key factor in setting in motion the Inquisition in the late 1500s and what would eventually become the Holocaust with the rise of the Nazis in the 1930s and 40s? Such were the questions I had that have been satisfied only in part over the years. Wonder and curiosity and skepticism and interest in all things spiritual remain very much a part of my journey into the mysteries of the divine still today.

It was a particularly lovely Sunday when my wife and I were driving through the countryside of Austria, meandering our way down from Prague, heading toward Salzburg. Shortly after noon, we noted a small sign along the side of the road, pointing to Mauthausen Concentration Camp. My eyebrows immediately went up. I had spent years in my thirties reading everything I could find on the Holocaust, after being introduced to William Shirer's *The Rise and Fall of the Third Reich* as a teenager. I had wanted to somehow figure out how things could have possibly gone so wrong. I wanted to better understand the social conditions that gave rise to such horrific abuses of power, as well as the psychology of individual development that would lead to torture and murder and disregard for human life on such a massive scale. It was almost too large to grasp in any meaningful way, overwhelming and despair-inducing. Still, I realized I could not do my work, which was essentially *caring* for hurting people, without getting a deeper appreciation for what had happened.

We turned in toward the camp, and little did I know how what was to come would shape the rest of my life. I was struck, first of all, by the bucolic beauty—the tree-lined lane, the rolling hills, the warm and gentle sun lighting up the grain in the surrounding fields. As with so many things having to do with extreme violence and distortion, the disparity was stunning. And then, as we came up over the rise, all of a sudden multiple very large and contemporary iron statues came into view, erected on the ledge of the deep rock quarry, Mauthausen being a labor camp as well as a death camp. The first one we saw took my breath away and stopped me cold. It was thirty feet tall, made from black iron beams, a man standing firm, with head bowed and fisted arm raised. So powerful was that image that I remember deep and profound emotions welling up inside of me and I could barely move. I learned that it had been placed there by the country of Bulgaria, in honor of the thousands of their Jewish citizens that had labored in that quarry and then been murdered. There were another dozen statues, scattered along the hillside, all massive, all deeply evocative, all erected by countries who had suffered the death of their citizens in that horrible place.

Very slowly, we made our way through them and on into the camp. For an hour, I wandered alone, deep in my thoughts, struggling to maintain some equilibrium, wrestling with how to absorb what I was seeing and experiencing. I stood in the "medical lab" where "human experiments" were performed without anesthesia, the shelves lined with jars of human teeth and body parts. I walked through the spare and crowded barracks. I stood paralyzed in the gas chamber, sickened and stunned. I had the sense that I had to be there, realizing that it was necessary somehow for my own spiritual development to do so. But my God! And it took no imagination to experience the horror. Would I be able to integrate it? How could I work with the dissonance between what I was seeing and experiencing and what I had been taught about a dualistic religious world view? I took in the crematorium and the burial pits and then stopped to look out into the fields and tried to regain perspective. And I recalled reading Elie Wiesel's *Night*

and the passage about the young boy being hanged, seemingly as an amuse-
ment for the guards, and one of the observer's asking, "Where is God?" and
Wiesel, his faith shattered, responding "Where is God now? Where is He?
Here He is—He is hanging here on this gallows . . . ."[1]

There were probably five of us at the camp that afternoon, all nodding
silently to one another to acknowledge both each other's presence and that
what we were seeing was unspeakable. But then we heard some cars coming up the drive and turned to see three black official-looking limousines
arriving. Curious, we waited as the President of Israel (the third-ranking
position in the Israeli government, we were told) arrived for an unan-
nounced wreath-laying ceremony at the memorial in the central square.
He was accompanied by an Austrian news crew. We were an oddly-bonded
group of about twelve that gathered around that sacred memorial. In a quietly dignified manner, he laid the wreath, said a private prayer, and then
turned to the camera to speak. He did so in Hebrew. The news crew only
spoke German. We understood neither. Yet, as he spoke, his eyes filled with
tears. And then, slowly, so did the cameraman's and the reporter's and the
interpreter's. And then, so did ours. We stood there together, powerfully
connected to each other, united in our sorrow and horror and grief.

Spiritual intelligence is built on understanding our history and development, even when no clear understanding is possible. Humankind's
history of violence to itself is one of the painful consequences of having
evolved as the strongest and most intelligent of the species. And the treatment of the Jewish people, in particular, by supposedly Christian churches
and governments, is one of the most horrifying and evil expressions of
all human history. It was both active and passive; to know what was happening and to do nothing was as evil as participating in the atrocities. We
cannot embrace a meaningful and healthy spirituality without fully coming to grips with that history first, just as we struggle today in coming to
grips with our own history, here in America, of enslaving black people. The
unspeakable antisemitism and racism that has profoundly colored human
history for the last two thousand years, and perhaps far longer, illustrates
human limitation and "sin" better than anything else. And perhaps its worst
expression is when it is clothed in righteousness. For the last two thousand
years, just as there have been deeply spiritually attuned compassionate and
justice-oriented expressions, so have there been fundamentalists—at the

1. Wiesel, *Night*, 62.

same time—who become caught up in rigid exclusivity and discrimination or, worse, destructive oppression.

Though there are plenty of sources suggesting discrimination against Jewish communities in ancient time, it is the evolving dogmatism of the early Christian church that suggest the strongest foundations for early antisemitism. In approximately 140 CE, at a time when the distinctions between Judaism and early Christianity were still blurred, with rival sects competing for adherents, Justin Martyr, among others, vilified the Jews in an attempt to prevent non-Jews from embracing the Torah, setting the tone for what was to come. In a particularly ugly charge made for political gain, he alleged that Jews were guilty of persecuting Christians and had done so ever since they "had killed the Christ."

It caught on, with Justin and then Tertullian, both renowned theologians, setting in motion the popular misconception that it was the "synagogues of the Jews" that became "fountains of persecution." The Big Lie was taking hold. It is interesting to me that they are the individuals remembered by a distorted history as brilliant churchmen, rather than those who taught the ethic of the gospel faithfully, without any such recognition. Clearly, the spirituality of the early church receded as those using it for control gained power. It was anything but inclusive, and obedience to official definitions of the new religion became the order of the day, complete with establishing a dualistic world view that included the threat of eternal damnation, and ensuring that certain gospel accounts (e.g. the gospel of Thomas) that might sew confusion, were excluded from the scriptural canon. The stereotypes promulgated by the fundamentalists shaped Christian attitudes toward Jews from late antiquity all the way into the medieval period, leading in fact, to periodic outbreaks of Christians violently persecuting the Jews.

It may be important to note *why* the Jewish people were resented and oppressed by the dominant culture. Most scholars would say—though this is grossly reductionistic—that it is likely because they tended toward being shopkeepers and moneylenders, having been forbidden for more than a millennium from doing anything else. Through the centuries of the "dark ages," the "serf and master" structure was deemed righteous by The Church, and power was closely guarded. As a result, the Jewish people had to set up their own self-sustaining shops and local businesses in order to survive and maintain a community, and they were, simply, resented for it. And then, as the notion of Jesus being "God" spread throughout the Roman Empire, especially with the politically expedient "conversion" of Constantine to the

Christian faith in 312, they were falsely accused of deicide, the ultimate slander.

If anything, antisemitism has been on the rise again these last years, as nationalistic ideologies have proliferated. On the far right, white supremacists have been quick to project their own time-honored fantasies and conspiracy theories of Jewish power and malfeasance onto contemporary events, however irrelevant. This became quickly apparent in August of 2017 as an intense debate arose around statues that glorified the Generals of the American Confederacy during the Civil War—which had been fought to defend slavery—the debate being driven forward by the Black Lives Matter movement. At Charlottesville, Virginia, white-supremacist and racist demonstrators protesting against the removal of a statue of Confederate General Robert E. Lee began chanting "Jews will not replace us," an apparent reference to the conspiratorial belief that "Jewish Communists" were running the city government. The demonstration gained tacit approval from Donald Trump, and antisemitic incidents have increased every year since. Seeing the insurrectionists who overran the Capital building on 1/6/21, wearing shirts emblazoned with "Camp Auschwitz" and "Work Brings Freedom"—the cynical lie above the entrance to Auschwitz—and other antisemitic and racist slurs, shows that such hate, now in alliance with fundamental Christianity and the culture of Trumpism, is continuing to raise its ugly head.

It wasn't just the Jews that the early Christian fundamentalists vilified. As Christianity grew from small community-based sects into the official religion of the Holy Roman Empire, steps were taken to oppress and eliminate all other religious expressions as well. In 392 AD, the Emperor Theodosius outlawed the rapidly growing religious group that had no formal name and is referred to in most accounts as the "Mysteries."[2] That movement was based in Eleusis, Greece, which had become a pilgrimage sight for hundreds of thousands of people, who traveled from all over Asia Minor to participate in their rituals. And, notably, the rituals and the temple were led by women. In short order, Bishop Theophilus (Greek for "beloved of God") of Alexandria led a rabid mob into what had been called "the most beautiful building in the world" and razed it to the ground, in part because the temple also contained a statue of the Greco-Egyptian god Serapis, the god who represented divine majesty, fertility and healing in the non-Christian world.

---

2. Muraresku, *The Immortality Key*, 26.

The loss, according to scholars, was unimaginable, since the temple was also a library, and contained the greatest collection (hundreds of thousands of volumes) of ancient Greek writings anywhere. Our knowledge of the culture and history of ancient Greece was reduced to about ten percent of what we might have known had the temple not been destroyed. An additional two thousand statues, shrines and temples were also destroyed across Greece in the purge. And then Theophilus built a church on the ruins of the temple, dedicated to John the Baptist.

For a period of several hundred years after the Church became established, turmoil and violence ensued right alongside the progression and expansion of the Christian faith, a profound cultural phenomenon. And again, it wasn't just the Jews and the Greeks that were targeted. Anyone seen as a challenge to the domination systems being put in place was vulnerable. Riane Eisler, in her influential book published back in the late '80s entitled *The Chalice and the Blade*, details how gender distinctions, especially, were aligned with the historical shift from collaborative cultures to patriarchal cultures, and how women tended to become subjugated to male power and control. For example, as the male-led church became established throughout Europe, tolerance for female-led pagan worship communities dropped precipitously, especially in France, and hundreds of women, now labeled as witches or some other pejorative term, were subsequently slaughtered.

We humans are clearly capable of both great good and great destruction, of both great love and great hate. We have evolved incredible capacities to reason, understand, perceive and interpret. We have unlocked the secrets of the stars and of the atom, but we have not yet mastered how to live in harmony with one another. Power and money are highly addictive drugs, and as we have developed the abilities to use them well to the benefit of all, so have we developed the capacities for using them to discriminate, diminish and destroy. We have the wisdom to manage those qualities and to set them in a spirituality that enhances life, but so also do we preclude such wisdom for those who follow us by our expressions of hate and abuse. Indeed, many theorists suggest that such psychic pain is unconsciously inherited. We carry within our psyches the compendium of hurt and trauma suffered by all those who have gone before. We have learned that traumatic experiences and boundary violations and verbal diminishment suffered as children can lead to toxic narcissism and sociopathy. And we know that such unresolved woundedness, often deeply repressed out of conscious awareness, precludes any meaningful spiritual development without compassionate intervention.

So, it is critical that we find ways to both confront destructive expressions and to engage each other with empathy and love, to both hold violators accountable and to seek to reform the cultural manifestations that drive them (note, for instance, the years-long process of the contemporary Catholic Church to identify and remove the thousands of priests caught up in the sexual abuse scandal, and to attempt to provide some form of compensation for the victims). It is imperative that we teach each other and empower one another to get renewed perspective and to make meaning by exploring the sacred stories and texts of our collective oral traditions that have created the pathways for getting outside of ourselves in order that we might develop an appreciation for the healing energies that flow around us and within us, seeking our wholeness.

Perhaps the early Christian fundamentalists were reflecting their Roman masters. The Romans were every bit as ruthless and destructive as the Nazis, if also more creative. They built the most powerful war machine the world had seen to that time, and for five hundred years of our history they expanded their empire by dominating, imprisoning, crucifying and enslaving all who were in their way. They also created incredibly advanced engineering marvels, beautiful art, glorious amphitheaters and coliseums and mansions, and temples that were dedicated to their gods. Theirs was a spiritual belief system based on strength, power and appeasement, not on any morality that promoted the greater good or community benefit, at least not for anyone other than their own ruling class. And they expanded their empire wherever it was profitable to do so. One of those areas was the middle east, and in particular, Jerusalem.

In 63 BCE the Roman general Pompey conquered and occupied Jerusalem. The Romans largely allowed free religious practice in Judea, but over time the divide between monotheistic and polytheistic religious views, combined with the brutal oppression and the prolific use of crucifixion, led to Jewish uprisings and violent clashes. Oppressive taxation and dominating imperialism were in full force by the time of Jesus, and that context is critical in grasping who Jesus was and what he did.

❀❀❀❀❀

Ten years ago, I traveled with a group of clinical educators to Jerusalem, to consult with the Israeli *Reshet* (spiritual care network) in setting up a system for clinical spiritual care in their hospitals and care centers. As a part of that trip, we drove up to swim in the Dead Sea and visit the Jordan River. One of my colleagues asked if we would re-baptize him in the River Jordan, recalling the beautiful story at the beginning of Mark's gospel when John the Baptist did so to Jesus, with the voice of God booming from the heavens claiming Jesus as his son. We did so with joy and delight, with laughter and tears, utilizing those same words, acknowledging that we too had been chosen by the divine to do such sacred work.

We then drove on to the town of Tiberius and the Sea of Galilee, getting history lessons from our guide as we went. We walked through the low hills, just below the Golan Heights, recalling the stories about Jesus and his followers that occurred there—the stories of fishing and teaching and healing, including the feeding of the five thousand and the encounters with Mary Magdalene and the woman at the well. The moment that stays with me most powerfully was when we stood on a rise above the lake and the guide told the story about Jesus, from the gospel of Luke, making his decision to go to Jerusalem, most likely to protest and confront the authorities, both Roman and Jewish, the Romans for their oppressive tactics and abuses, and the Jewish Pharisees for their compliance and complicity. Recalling and reprising the text from Isaiah in the Hebrew scriptures, Luke wrote that Jesus turned to look toward Jerusalem, some forty miles away, and "set his face like a flint," meaning with clear and sharply defined intentionality, no matter the consequences. It was a powerful moment for us as we began to get in touch with the courage required—and with the power needed and costs suffered—of confronting the oppressors. And my spiritual intelligence was deepened once again.

So, who actually was Jesus, really? By this time, according to most historians and scholars, Jesus was likely aligned with the Zealots, a group of Jewish activists doing all they could to throw off the yoke of Roman oppression. Yet, his clear focus was on doing things differently. Jesus was, by all accounts, a brilliant scholar and a profoundly charismatic (in the best sense of the word) and influential teacher and rabbi, if also seen by the establishment (the Pharisees) as a radical and as something of an outlier. His teaching often challenged Jewish precepts, recognizing and exposing the distortions that had crept in over the centuries, always calling the faithful back to the core spirituality of the Torah that was life-giving and community-enhancing. And his teaching never strayed from its core expression of love, both divine love from "the Father" and loving words and actions toward one another as the dominant ethic for life. There was no room for violence, from his perspective, and no room for falsehoods, hatred and abuses of personal authority either. He preached authenticity, transparency and vulnerability, in the sense of presenting oneself as open-hearted and compassionate, while also being direct, prophetic and confrontive of human abuses. He was the progenitor of non-violent civil disobedience, influencing and shaping the work not only of his contemporaries but of prophetic leaders throughout history, most notably Ghandi and King in the last century. And he taught that taking that road less traveled had a greater intrinsic reward than any worldly victory could ever bring, that we come into the fullness of life when we serve one another *self-sacrificially*—a beautiful definition, I would suggest, of what we mean by the term "spirituality."

A few years back, my wife and I traveled again to Scotland, a favorite destination. This time we drove out onto the west coast island of Mull, in the Inner Hebrides, and then took the ferry across to the small (and carless) island of Iona. The abbey there had been established by St. Columba in 563, and Iona today is seen as the birthplace of Celtic Christianity and has become a popular destination for spiritual retreats, of which our visit would be yet one more. We arrived just in time for the vespers service in the beautiful stone abbey and I was fascinated to learn that the speaker providing the homily would be a Jewish rabbi and scholar from Harvard University. And he surprised me by speaking—with great erudition—on a gospel text from the Christian scriptures, beautifully explicating the ministry of Jesus and moving us all to a profound sense of oneness, with a holy and timeless message. In that moment, I was again provided what I was seeking, and my spirituality and appreciation for unity and diversity expanded and deepened accordingly.

Did Jesus suspect that he might very well lose his own life, as he traveled to Jerusalem? I imagine so, just as King did when he gave his last speech in Memphis stating that he had already "been to the mountaintop" and that traveling further down the road "really didn't matter to (him) now"; just as John Lewis suspected he might when he led the marchers across the Edmund Pettis bridge only to have his skull cracked-open; just as Gandhi did when he was beaten while leading protests against racism in South Africa and then again later, against British imperialism in India. Jesus entered Jerusalem not as a populist movement leader on a white horse, but as a defiantly humble and reflective leader, calling out the corrupt rulers of the city, both Roman and Jewish, by riding a small donkey, a symbol of lowliness and unworthiness. I suspect when he gathered with his friends to honor the Passover and eat and drink together, he could fully imagine the events to come, and his likely suffering and death. He wasn't being impulsively foolish; he was being consistent and true to his principles, doing what was necessary to change hearts and minds. Did he have any idea how his thoughts and actions would change history? I doubt it; but I also suspect he knew fully well how they would fill his own heart and further the cause of challenging Roman oppression while teaching an ethic of both non-violent protest and self-sacrifice.

Due in part to losing the emphasis on Jesus' teaching and witness, the mainstream church today is in a slow but steady decline. While some congregations, both protestant and Catholic, are refocusing their messages toward a new emphasis on healthy spirituality and communal love and justice, and beginning to grow and proliferate, others remain mired in the status quo. While a new "reformation" of sorts appears to be gathering across the country and in much of Europe, with a focus less on beliefs and more on living in caring and prayer-centered communities, with people who seem to desire tempering the materialism and strife of our current culture with meaningful connections and expanded mindfulness, most still seem committed to holding tightly to the tradition. America is clearly becoming more secular, while new inclusive faith communities, connected on-line and led by thoughtful progressives, seem to be, if not thriving, then slowly attracting reflective and autonomous people. The commitment to social justice and to care of the earth and its climate seem to be significant motivating factors in this shift.

But unfortunately, today's conservative evangelical churches are so far not a part of the reorientation, seemingly content with their large numbers and legalistic frameworks and, at least in the mega-churches, relatively anonymous worship. They are also, sadly, far from the teachings of Jesus. It is a fascinating dynamic in our culture that while they have diminished the ethic of the Christian gospel, their focus on "salvation" and on the concept of the resurrected Christ has become dominant. Alas, to do the latter without the former creates something of an empty spirituality. Perhaps as a result, key leaders in the conservative evangelical movement have too often given themselves over to the lure of power, sex, money and manipulation, especially in the last two decades.

Exploring and understanding the teachings and witness of Jesus is, I suggest, a key step in developing greater spiritual intelligence for everyone.

The image of Jesus, working to transform the hearts of the oppressors through a transcendent expression of love, has become an archetype. As a Jew and an educated rabbi under Roman rule, his authoritative message of non-violent resistance combined with a profound commitment to inclusivity and love for all humanity, shook the foundations of human culture. And he taught timeless perspectives with wisdom and insight and influence. Whether religious or not, whether "Christian" or not, exploring his teachings and getting a handle on his witness to the authorities of both temple and state, shapes and informs us in how to live meaningful and fulfilling lives. Indeed, his life and ministry, as represented by multiple writers, reveals a universal truth that transcends all attempts to dogmatize it.

As we slowly—through research and scholarship—got inside Jesus' teachings and inside the witness of the early church, we began to get the image of someone amazingly and powerfully attuned to the influx of divine energy and aware of the effects of how acting against inner feelings and stirrings could only lead to emptiness and futility. It has changed things remarkably, and turned us back from an emphasis on the messianic mission of the Christ figure to a richly impactful lifting up and amplification of what he had to *say*. It was his *message* that "saved" people from themselves. It was his example, his way of being, his insight and perspective and ability to capture and represent what appeared to be divine intent that had the profound impact.

The early Christian messaging around Jesus' death got distorted as well, into the concept of atonement (Jesus dying as expiation for the sins of the world) and of his "resurrection" that somehow became the pathway to eternal life (for believers only), burying the liberating value of his teachings. It was those *teachings*, the ones about unconditional love and self-sacrificial service, that changed the world, not the projection of his messianic identity. When Albert Schweitzer introduced his seminal work, *The Quest of the Historical Jesus* in 1906, it introduced the distinction between the "Christ of Faith" and the "Jesus of History." Throughout most of Christian history, the former concept won the day, with an emphasis on Jesus' "divine" nature and messianic purpose. Unfortunately, the mystique that rose up around Jesus over the centuries divorced the "Christ-ian" religion from who Jesus really was, and perhaps more importantly, from the profound message of his teachings and witness. Following Schweitzer and the work of many dedicated scholars, the more progressive writers and teachers of current Christian expression are now lifting up a spirituality and way of life that more accurately reflects the original experiences and messages and ethic of the historical Jesus and his contemporaries.

I'm reminded of the words of Marcus Borg, the wonderful historian and theologian. In a lecture I attended some years before his death, Borg said this about the person and ministry of Jesus: "Surely, Jesus was one of the two most impressive and influential individuals in all human history," articulating that he, along with Gautama Buddha in Asia, had greater influence on every aspect of human life from his historical time to the present, than anyone else in history. And here I am, writing about Jesus as still shaping spiritual intelligence, some two thousand years later.

Indeed, perhaps the key struggle in the recent evolution of Christian faith and spirituality has been to clarify and comprehend what the church embraced and espoused early on regarding the divine nature of Jesus, and then to reinterpret it for today. In the confessions of our Christian churches, whether left, right or center, Jesus was indeed proclaimed as "both God and man" and as "the Christ" and as the "son of God." He was perceived in the early church as having been "raised from the dead" in the resurrection, and as having "ascended" into the "kingdom of heaven" as benevolent and loving ruler, and was anticipated to return to earth again at "the end times" to save all who believed in him. But the construction and advancement of Jesus as God was expressive of a dualistic framework (good vs evil; God "up" there, us down here) that seemed to blur out his deeply empowered and attuned humanity. Those aspects of the gospel story that heightened Jesus' godly qualities seemed to relegate his teaching and his life example to the back burner. The Apostle's and Nicene creeds were then written to capture and promote that divine perspective, and they remain definitive in the tradition. Yet it is apparent that these core defining elements of Christianity were prompted as much by political expediency as by a deep faith in the chroniclers of Jesus' life, and the creeds weren't even written until the first half of fourth century, amidst massive social and political reorganization.

Today, as progressive churches have wrestled with the lessons of the Holocaust and two world wars, and as they have slowly and quietly embraced contemporary and science-based theologies and eastern religious influences, and as evangelical churches have, on the other hand, ignored their own core beliefs in favor of political influence and the gospel of personal happiness and success, that original core emphasis on Jesus as Messiah and as dying for the sins of the world has lost stature. The traditional message of the gospel, still reflective of first century thinking and scientific knowledge, just doesn't seem to capture the interests of thoughtful, educated people today. Unfortunately, that shift in core beliefs has also dragged down the essence of Christian spirituality. Perhaps it is fair to say that the tradition no longer has sway over modern life for most, as America becomes continuously more secular, now with—for the first time—just over half of the American public saying they are no longer religious.

And yet, as noted earlier, something powerful is indeed stirring. In smaller groups the world over, we are seeing the rising up of a new spirituality that incorporates higher consciousness and scientific reality, taking Jesus' teachings to a more expansive and engaging place. And the spirituality of self-sacrificial love that has been compromised by all the competing values of an anxious world, is evolving toward something new as well, as we recognize the threats posed by autocratic rulers and rapid climate change. Perhaps that is a natural evolution in consciousness. Perhaps, as new spiritual movements promoting Jesus' core message as consistent with raised awareness rise up to once again challenge the prevalent domination systems, this renaissance will gain momentum.

So, it is important to note that the life and ministry of Jesus clearly touched a universal nerve. He apparently had an amazing capacity for getting inside people's heads and hearts, for prompting a different vision, a change of expectation, a willingness to reorient toward a new way of being. He somehow elicited a higher consciousness in his hearers, struck by his insight and his engagement and his wisdom—and by his profound and convicting emphasis on compassionate love as the defining quality of spirituality. As best we can tell, his ethic of self-sacrificial love as the pathway toward personal meaning and fulfillment, as transcendent of normal human thought, stunned people and stopped them in their tracks. "Were not our hearts burning within us?" the travelers on the road to Emmaus were described as saying.[3] Having witnessed how he died, even the Roman Centurion overseeing his crucifixion is quoted as being so moved as to say, "Truly this man was God's son."[4] That we even today have similar experiences, moved to a deepened faith when encountered by the gospel stories, is a testament to their power, and to the eternal truth of their message. Surely, in that sense, Jesus is very much "present" in this hurting world.

And yet we don't really know who Jesus was, other than what was portrayed through the gospels—and they are very human documents. We

3. NRSV, Luke 24:32.
4. NRSV, Mark 15:39.

have no eyewitness accounts. We have no contemporary written histories; if there were any, they have been lost. And the gospels, which serve as our best source, were written well after Jesus lived, reflecting the social changes occurring in the intervening years. Mark, the earliest of the gospels, was written somewhere between 60 and 70 CE, some thirty-plus years after the crucifixion. Matthew and Luke were written in the 80s, notably following the destruction of the Jewish temple in Jerusalem by the Romans which changed the social and political landscape drastically. And then John was written likely between 100 and 110, three generations after Jesus. None of them were written as factually accurate historical accounts; all were written with their own distinctive perspectives and in unique social and political situations. Mark was written primarily to fulfill the prophecy of a suffering servant who would raise apocalyptic expectations for oppressed and marginalized Gentiles. It was intended as a message of "good news" and hope, written for a community of Gentile Christians living in Rome, directly under the thumb of the emperor. It centered as much on expectations of "deliverance from oppression" as on the image of the empty tomb, and what that might mean.

In the original ending of Mark's gospel, in fact, there were no post-resurrection appearances, as were added much later in the other gospels. Indeed, the image of the empty tomb was likely included in Mark to strengthen the faith of those who were already moved by Jesus' teachings and ministry. Matthew and Luke both took Mark's gospel and added and subtracted material, crafting it to fit their particular circumstances and messages, both writing about the same stories with different details and emphases and then each including some unique stories as well. Matthew's audience was a community of Jewish Christians living in Roman-occupied Syria. His work reflects the sharp divide between those Jews who accepted Jesus as the Messiah and those who did not. Luke was written for a small community of educated and Greek-speaking Jesus-followers as a text to encourage their faith and promote the universality of Jesus' message. John, written later, was composed not so much to give an overview of the life and ministry of Jesus as to encourage a Jewish-Gentile community outside of Palestine to focus on his post-ascension reign. John is a beautifully poetic and imaginative gospel, promoting Jesus as the Messiah, the one whom he understood was the definitive revelation of God. Each of the four gospels eventually included in the canon of scripture (among the many written) were meant to tell a story of *faith*, not provide a historically accurate narrative.

The birth narratives, the miracle stories, the narratives of the crucifixion and resurrection and post-resurrection—all differed in the gospels, and all were written not as eyewitness accounts, but as orally-preserved stories and homiletical metaphors. They were meant to symbolically instill an evocative future vision and a deep spiritual hope that promised that deliverance from oppression would come through faith in what the one who fully captured and embodied the essence of the divine represented. The authors of the gospels were in fact brilliant writers, using metaphor and symbolism and subtle emphases on key teachings and expressions to rally a new way of being and a higher spiritual consciousness in a world deep in conflict and political oppression. Their staying power has been remarkable. That a new religion sprang from their words to become a world-changing way of being still today, is beyond remarkable. No wonder the Christian faith proclaims the scriptures to be divinely inspired.

Indeed, as a spiritual person, I hold to the deep and abiding sense that Jesus was fully human and yet somehow, also, fully able to capture and reflect the divine. Ah, but . . . It doesn't make sense to say that he was different from us in substance, but yet he was clearly remarkable, a singular figure. How could it be that he seemed to have manifested and embodied the divine spirit in ways that no one else ever had, at least no one else known to us? How did he become so attuned, so conscious of the inherent dynamics of living fully into that spirit that he captured the imaginations not only of his contemporaries but of generation after generation to come? Was he the definitive revelation of God, or was he somehow invited into what we are all invited into—a just life of self-sacrificial love and service? Such questions lead us into the arenas of anthropology, of science and theology, including what is usually referred to as *quantum* theology (based on what we are learning from quantum physics), which seeks to understand and contextualize the flow of energy that animates us all, and that tunes us into creative and meaningful—and *loving*—ways of being in the world. Indeed, it may be that Jesus' divine qualities are reflective of what we might now understand as heightened consciousness and as having a higher frequency of cosmic energy that is built into all of creation—and built into us as well.

Chapter Four

Learning to Love the Learning

"Human beings are poor examiners, subject to superstition, bias, prejudice, and a profound tendency to see what they want to see rather than what is really there."

—M. SCOTT PECK, *THE ROAD LESS TRAVELED*

WE HUMAN BEINGS ARE fascinating, wondrous creatures. From our very beginning some 200,000 years ago when there were five distinct species of us, we have been, by nature, creators and imaginers, seekers and explorers. Our brains have continued to evolve into extremely complex mechanisms that not only make it possible for us to self-regulate and define ingenious ways to survive, but also to perceive and intuit and develop a conscious appreciation of our world, our universe, and our subliminal connections within and without. We have always sought new experiences, new connections, and deepened understanding.

Since the very beginning, we have created gods to assuage our struggles with meaning-making, to have something beyond our own human incapacities to believe in. We have evolved countless creation myths and redemption stories, and a myriad of divine images to guide our expressions over the millennia, to transcend our circumstances and to provide feelings of hope and joy.

As our ancient communities grew and multiplied, and as our brains developed and grew more complex, and as our consciousness of an expanded world enhanced our perspectives and awareness, so did our ability to sustain ourselves and to collaborate with each other and to form moral constructs to help make meaning and organize our lifestyles. And the central component of that process of meaning-making was wondering about and reflecting on the nature of life itself, and on what it was that provided the rains and the warmth and the seasons, that occupied and put in motion the heavens and the stars, that brought life out of the womb and then took it back again, that provided courage in battle and patience in struggle and hope when all seemed hopeless. It is an incredible story.

Most every culture evolved its own mythologies and its own way of ordering spiritual rituals and events as well. Most did so by appointing the wise ones, the seers and mystics and shamans and priests, to both directly connect to the divine and to then interpret their experiences for their people. Some became prophets, some teachers, some healers, some wise philosophers and, alas, some tyrants. Recent research, by Yuval Harari and others, reveals that it is likely that most of the shamans in ancient hunter-gatherer cultures were profoundly influential in the success or failure of the tribal communities they led, and that they were both male and female. It is also fascinating that the profound spiritual experiences they had were likely stimulated as much by natural psychedelics that occurred in plants and fungi—the psilocybin found in some mushrooms, the mind expanding chemicals in peyote, the LSD that occurs naturally in the fungus *ergot* that grows on barley—as by their perceptions of liminal experiences and their wonder at the natural world.

Brian Muraresku, again in his book *The Immortality Key*, details the fascinating experiences of awe and connection and beloved-ness that resulted from the psychoactive chemicals ingested, whether intentionally or not, conclusions that are supported by the current and ongoing psychedelic studies at Johns Hopkins University in Baltimore. It is those chemicals that are likely the source for many of the ancient fanciful and visionary cave paintings discovered on the European continent, as well as for the formation of many of the lasting rituals that we have inherited. In fact, the modern day Christian sacrament of communion (the Eucharist) may have evolved in the earliest years of what would become the Christian Church out of not only the Jewish Passover meal but also the much older tradition of gathering into small communal groups, led by the shaman, to "eat and drink" a psychoactive substance, in order to elicit an ecstatic spiritual experience. Fascinating.

As our self-understanding grew over time, so did our god images change and evolve. As ancient tribes traveled to new lands and developed more advanced cultures, so did they develop new god images as well. Some developed images of an all-powerful sky god, while others developed feminine, nurturing, earth-based goddess images. Still others—the Norse, the Greeks, the Romans, the Egyptians, some Asian cultures—developed an entire panoply of gods who offset or complemented or competed with one another and with humankind as well. Some had a deep sense of reverence and appreciation of the sacred, while others developed more pragmatic and powerful images as a projection of their own challenging circumstances. And as the god images changed to suit social experiences and circumstances, so did a wide variety of rituals get created to mark the key events of birth and maturation and marriage and death, and on and on. They were and are an attempt to bring the experience of the divine into the present moment, and to bless somehow the process of becoming, of loss and heartbreak, of beginning anew, of growth and connection, and ultimately of quietly coming to an end. We are a people who seek meaning and understanding, who seek to make sense of our experiences and then to repeat the good ones as often as possible.

It is human nature, however (and an inherent trait of being autonomous individuals), to bend such images and rituals and experiences toward our own needs and desires, of course. Our fears and anxieties and vulnerabilities would play out in efforts to protect ourselves and to limit the influences of others. It was a natural evolutionary process, then, for all those images and rituals to become distorted or co-opted by some as a way to gain and use power. As noted, our history is filled with such distortions leading to social abuses and attempts to control, or worse, to conflict and killing. Warrior cultures which honored the Great Spirit would also call on that same spirit to empower the slaughter of enemies. Male-dominated cultures would subjugate women in the name of appeasing the gods or honoring the sky god's demands. Over and over, the holy would give way to the profane, and we would distort our original intent. And that certainly is not only an ancient phenomenon; think of Bob Dylan's lament about the war in Viet Nam entitled "With God On Our Side," a reprise from Psalm 108:13.

The story that gave rise to the religion of Christianity—the story of Jesus' influence—has shaped our spiritual narratives more than any other here in the West, though like all stories of our history, it has been altered again and again, both knowingly and unknowingly, to serve political expediency.

That was perhaps inevitable because it was born out of political and social struggle itself. Yet so powerful has this story been that it has shaped whole cultures and deeply embedded itself into the hearts and minds of hundreds of millions of us. And as it evolved, it became a still more multi-layered story of both goodness and tragedy, of both the light and the dark, of both despair and hope. And it, too, has been tragically and deeply distorted.

We have forever asked the questions of ourselves, "What do we need to know to live a full and meaningful life? What should guide us and motivate us and shape our ways of being? What do we need to learn?" *How, then, shall we live?* It's in Ecclesiastes in the Hebrew scriptures and in Luke's gospel and in one of Peter's letters in the Christian scriptures as well. Indeed, it's the universal question: what should I do, how should I be, who should I be with, where should I go, what does this or that mean, *how should I then live*?

As seekers and wonderers, it is the unique experience of the human species to ponder and ask such questions, indeed, to face our experiences and feelings of being anxious or confused or overwhelmed *reflectively*, that is, to consider thoughtfully how to express ourselves most productively and meaningfully in the face of challenging realities. Over the centuries, we have constructed values and guidelines and moral frameworks to guide and capture those ways of being that seem most likely to generate positive experiences for ourselves and others in the human community, that provide both extrinsic and *intrinsic* reward, from the Golden Rule and the Beatitudes to the Nuremburg Code and the Seven Habits of Highly Successful People. Each new iteration expands and deepens our awareness and capacity to live a more meaningful life. And the process continues. With each shift in the subcultures of human society, and with each new social upheaval or personal struggle, we re-ask the questions again. And of course, there is no one right answer; they ebb and flow for every one of us. But there does seem to be a near-uniform recognition of what *must* happen to live well, and that is to take in and consider and embed new information.

Indeed, spiritual intelligence infers openness to learning—the process of moving toward deepened understanding, toward becoming better attuned to the deeper, sometimes hidden, realities of life. We need to *learn*, because to learn is to begin to see new things and to see old things in a new light; it is to begin to perceive and tune-in in new ways. How can we be consciously awakened to the processes that give us life and lift our spirits and soften our hearts and inspire our ideas and give rise to our expressions of love and joy without learning about what is actually happening?

We deepen our souls when we learn, for instance, about the workings of the brain and the energy in the universe and the components of consciousness, and when we draw from the insights of the great philosophers and theologians and scholars and scientists and poets and teachers who have gone before and of those who today chart our way. "Learning is everything," as Mark Twain once said. The process of taking in new information, mulling it over, throwing out old concepts that no longer fit the emerging reality, gaining a new awareness and higher consciousness—that is learning. And it is the essential mechanism for spiritual growth and deepening meaning, for understanding and managing our responses to things, both cognitive and emotional. And there is so much to learn!

We are currently in what many reflectors and pundits refer to as "the post-truth era." What has come to be referred to as "fake" news abounds, in the specious efforts of power seekers to distort reality and influence political views, in personal fabrications spread on social media, in cable television programming and for-profit radio. Political leaders, seeking to sway public opinion, label real information and science-based facts as fake, and promote false information and outright lies as real. Timothy Snyder's profoundly influential article entitled "The American Abyss"[1] in the New York Times, describes how such dynamics play into the emergence of fascism. It's a dangerous game playing out in political circles because many of the issues being distorted have long-term ramifications for Americans and, indeed, for the future of humankind. And, perhaps most importantly, the cognitive dissonance it sets up is dispiriting. We feel less together, less integrated.

Now, more than ever it seems, we need to seek to learn and to try to discern the truth. We need to seek understanding and to attempt to make decisions based on reality and not on wishful thinking or political distortions. But we are a vulnerable people. Without reliable truth-based sources, we are prone to be swayed by dominant messages in our subcultures. Thus, we are confronted by the growing political and social divide.

In recent days I've had several conversations with casual friends and neighbors about the issues at play in our country—the coronavirus pandemic, the racial disparities, the economy, the presidential election. Two of my neighbors were making statements about current issues that were not

1. Snyder, *The American Abyss.*

accurate and, in one case, were abjectly false and based on made-up misinformation disseminated by an administrative spokesperson and a cable news network. I asked them both where they had gotten their information, and they both named a particular cable outlet. I gently asked who else they were reading or if they had done any research to learn about the issue. "No one" and "don't need to" were the answers. I realize this is not a foreign conversation to many who are reading this. I suspect we all know well people who remain uninformed and proudly so, maybe people even in our own families—people who make it a point of pride to *not* read legitimate news sources, and who become strongly self-defended and even hostile when challenged. It has become a heart-breaking reality for so many because we recognize that to stay spiritually attuned and alive, we need to take in new information and think it through. We need to actually *seek* understanding. To not do so is to become static, stuck, and one-dimensional, no matter how "religious," no matter how influential, no matter how well-connected to like-minded people. Indeed, the tribal coalescing of the right wing evangelical Christian church over the last couple decades has led to a morally rigid and uninformed coalition of congregations and spiritually-distorted clergy.

What we are talking about here is learning to become more fully human, learning to deepen our hearts and expand our minds, learning to grow. Indeed, learning is everything. And it is perhaps critical to realize that we learn best, not by seeking information that reinforces what we already believe to be true, but by attempting to *disprove* our knowledge, drawing firmer conclusions as a result. Those who seek new information and insight and understanding, and then who examine it and test it, grow and deepen as human beings. They develop their souls, if you will. To take in new learning is to collaborate with the divine spirit that somehow places the information in front of us as an offer that can lead to a fuller experience. It's a beautiful way of perceiving how we might live more fully, inviting deep listening and intuitive perception and fullness of feeling and then honoring our freedom to make our own choices. And as we do, we learn, becoming more aware, more astute, more perceptive, more alive, with each choice made. We feel more connected, less alone, as if we are partnering with the divine in a way that is mutually meaningful and filled with potential. Learning about such ways of thinking and perceiving, about ourselves and about our world, is everything, and it's the first step toward spiritual intelligence.

Cheri was 25 years old when she came for her training in the medical center where I was teaching. She was an African American single woman, preparing herself for parish ministry in a mainstream denomination. She had been raised in a middle-class suburb neighborhood of Los Angeles and was deeply familiar with the social dynamics of racism, white privilege, and the struggle for justice. And she had repeatedly experienced marginalization and diminishment as a woman seeking professional standing in the very conservative, evangelical Baptist tradition in which she was raised. While in college, she looked for a church with a more progressive theology and polity, in hopes of continuing the work of forerunners like Martin Luther King and Howard Thurman, and of contemporary black theologians like Emilie Townes and Teresa Fry Brown and William Barber. She presented as both defiant and over-confident, however, and it was clear that she had internal work to do. Her challenge would be to soften her edges without losing her prophetic voice, to learn to engage her patients directly but humbly and compassionately—most particularly the white male patient—and to grow into an *integrated* personal authority to embrace her full potential. When I asked Cheri to look at her defiance and rough edges, she initially balked, but then she started to talk about the abuse she had suffered at the hands of her "righteous" father, and about her self-doubts and fears of not being able to measure up, and her learning began to take on new and transformative depth.

Jordan was a 45 year old, highly successful white pastor in a mainstream denomination, now serving as the Senior Minister at a large and growing parish in a fairly conservative suburb of St. Louis, one of the growing number of mega-churches. He was married with a daughter in college and a teenager at home. He had a popular radio ministry and had written a successful devotional book and, by all measures, he was at the peak of his career. He was handsome, with an engaging smile and a winning personality. However, Jordan had been deeply closeted as a gay man, at a time when the mainstream churches still did not accept openly gay people, much less gay clergy. He had been "outed" after being seen with another man in a neighboring city. He subsequently came to us after being suspended from his position and sidelined by his district authority, hoping to redirect and resurrect his career. At the beginning of the interview process, he hid behind his persona, minimizing the impact of recent events, maintaining a certain bravado and false charm. I certainly didn't blame him, and I felt compassion for what he had been through. But now was not the time for inauthenticity. Jordan would quickly learn that his primary task would be to embrace his true identity, become authentic in his expressions, and integrate his story as a resource for his future ministry, trusting that the journey forward would be soul-sustaining. When I gently confronted him with how he was living a "divided life," he dropped his head and wiped his eyes and slowly responded, "Yes; and I want to learn how to be whole."

The focus of our learning initially needs to be on our own processes of *early* development—how our ways of thinking and feeling were influenced and shaped, both for good and for ill, by our own parents; how our ways of perceiving and synthesizing the words and actions of others could lead to powerful and overwhelming emotions, how our reactions to others can become either self-limiting or self-enhancing. In "family systems" psychology, we say that the process of *individuation* is essential for emancipating ourselves from unconscious parental controls, and is essential to developing the capacity to remain *differentiated* from those who might reflect the unresolved demands and expectations of our families. Developing spiritual intelligence turns on that process of furthering self-understanding, learning about human interactions, and better perceiving the movement of the divine spirit in the world. To explore such things openly and curiously and *intentionally*, is to continually make greater meaning, and it is a life-long quest for most of us.

It is no wonder, then, that I was drawn to the world of the interplay of psychology, religion, spirituality, medicine and ethics. Early on, I found I wanted to understand more fully the human condition and my own confusion, and how to respond to it positively and constructively. And it took considerable learning, all the way along, to get there.

For me, that process began as soon as my brain was able to absorb and reflect on new information. As children, our thoughts and ways of being are shaped by how our parents interact with us and by what they say and do (or don't do). It is a subtle and nuanced process with life-long ramifications that are most often kept unconscious. However, consciously "owning" the process of trying to figure things out, begins much later and is most often stimulated by painful experiences. When confronted with painful things in my childhood (the criticisms of others, put-downs and ridicule, my own screw-ups), my first response, typically, was usually one of felt inadequacy and withdrawal. Somehow, I would internalize reflexively that someone else had found me wanting, as not okay, as just plain *less than*, as not good enough or, worse, as defective. I, like most every child, didn't have the awareness at that stage of development to differentiate and validate myself when diminished. I merely felt bad.

Indeed, we have learned that children raised in disorganized families, or by a critical, scolding parent, tend to respond to painful episodes with feelings of shame and lowered self-esteem, something with which they may struggle throughout their lives. As impressionable kids, we absorbed both the positive and the negative influences that shaped our processes of becoming. Parents who were exhausted and depleted and who did not have the resourcefulness to apologize and reflect with and support the child later, unwittingly sparked problems socializing for their offspring. Though my family was fairly normal and healthy, that certainly fit my experience. And I ended up struggling with self-doubt and social anxiety throughout my adolescence and young adulthood, feelings that I didn't understand.

But slowly, during early adolescence, and because I was fortunate to have available resources and people who supported me, I resolved to learn, at first just to avoid being found wanting again, but gradually as a pathway toward self-empowerment. I was becoming individuated enough to want to understand what informed the behavior and expressions of others, particularly my parents and my classmates at school. It was something of a survival mechanism at the time, but gradually evolved into intentional learning about human behavior, and became a way to define myself and to stay differentiated in the face of harsh interactions. As a result, I was able to learn enough to be able to recognize that I would need to make my own way in the world, that I would need to learn more to build my skills and knowledge in order to be self-sufficient and to live life on my own terms. By late high school, I realized that only I could take responsibility for my sense of self and for how to live meaningfully, that just avoiding the criticism of others wasn't enough, but that I would do better to proactively join in collaborating with others to improve things for everyone. I was only haltingly successful at becoming the person I wanted to be. The grace was realizing that the same was true for most of us.

Not everyone was so fortunate. Not everyone is able to get the resources necessary to support integration, and not everyone is able on their own to synthesize the learning and adapt to difficult things. I loved being with my friend Jim in high school. He was seemingly everything I wasn't, in terms of casual self-confidence and athletic prowess and daring behaviors. He seemed always out on the edge somehow, pushing the boundaries, struggling with a practiced ease against the expectations of parents and teachers. He would be the first to try anything, and of course the girls found him fun-loving and attractive. I both envied him and felt concerned for him. But it was always exciting to be together, to get some cigarettes and go to the pool hall, to watch him throw snowballs at passing cars, or to just cruise the neighborhood, recklessly and daringly. He had a magnetic personality, and always seemed to be on the edge of trouble, which he would usually skate through, drawing on his disarming playfulness and big smile.

Reading some of the works of the Carl Jung, the great early psychologist, would eventually help me to understand our dual natures and how what he referred to as the "shadow"—our repressed psychic injuries—would unconsciously prompt our acting-out behaviors. Why was Jim so drawn to living on the edge? I slowly learned about his family, and that his father, who was in recovery and working as a "counselor," had been a "mean drunk" when Jim was young. I came to appreciate how Jim did not have much of a homelife, at least not one that he considered safe, and I came to understand later why he would always ask to meet me "on the corner" instead of inviting me to his house, or why he felt he needed to "sneak out" in order to join in on Saturday activities.

Slowly, things began to take a downward turn for him. By later college years, Jim wasn't much fun to be with anymore. His humor had taken on a sarcastic tone, he was more impulsive, his academic studies were up and down, and he was becoming isolated. Eventually, he spiraled down into heavy drinking and experimenting with other illegal substances. When he was twenty-five, he was still grounded enough to realize he needed help and he checked himself into a chemical dependency treatment center. I went to see him a couple of times, but it was difficult to connect; his shame and his reliance on his old bravado were distancing. It is a sad—though also pretty ordinary and common—story. He did manage to get sober, and he eventually became, like his father, a counselor in a treatment center in another state. I only saw him three or four times through the following years, always aware of feeling a tinge of sadness and helplessness. Jim did okay for the most part, staying successfully employed, but clearly life was hard. He married later in life, but when his wife died from breast cancer, it just seemed more than he could manage. His grief was deep, and he had been diagnosed with Parkinson's a couple years earlier, and he was still, alas, socially isolated. He wrote me a kind, if cryptic, email a few years ago, thanking me for being such a good friend way back when, and then closed by saying I wouldn't be hearing from him again. I was alarmed, responding with an invitation to try and get together, with all the heartfelt but somehow trivial-sounding words I could come up with. It went unanswered. And the following weekend, he ended his own life.

To manage life meaningfully and to enjoy it fully seems to require a certain sense of adaptability and resilience, which in turn, suggests a process of learning and renewal. As seekers and wonderers, we do not appear to do well when our spirituality and meaning-making processes get blocked by psychic injury.

Isn't the human story one of continual evolution and continual learning? Over the eons, we have progressively become more complex, more skilled, more adaptable, more attuned to emotions and feelings, more self-aware. As a species, we have become not only more intelligent beings, but wiser ones, more mindful, more perceptive, though it remains a paradox that so many seemingly choose not to use their capacities.

We are living at an incredible point in human history. Paralleling our individual journeys of learning and growing, our knowledge has literally exploded over the last seventy-five years. Since unlocking the secrets of the atom and of antibiotics and of DNA, we have been able to plumb the depths of the human body and brain as well as the depths of the oceans. We can now look not only into the farthest reaches of space, but into the smallest building blocks of life. We, seemingly, were born to learn, to explore, to create. And while we know that it is an innate trait of our species to attune to the divine mysteries and to respond with awe and gratitude, we are today seeing those mysteries as components of a unified whole, with science and theology coming together to speak with one voice. Old religious structures are dying away rapidly. A new consciousness is spreading across the globe. The challenge to each one of us is to open ourselves to that learning, to attune to the unfolding, and to align with that which feeds our spirit and deepens our souls.

Chapter Five

Opening Up

"Do not be dismayed by the brokenness of the world. All things break. And all things can be mended. Not with time, as they say, but with intention. So, go. Love intentionally, extravagantly, unconditionally. The broken world waits in darkness for the light that is you."

—L.R. KNOST, *THE GENTLE PARENT*

EMMANUEL CARRERE, THE FRENCH writer, tells the painfully beautiful story of living through the devastating 2004 Sri Lankan tsunami. He was vacationing there with his partner and their respective sons. They had been struggling with increasing distance and distress in their relationships, and following a particularly difficult discussion, decided against going down to the beach for their scheduled scuba diving lesson. Paradoxically, that decision saved both their lives and their care for one another. Two hours later, the most devastating tsunami in modern history hit. 35,000 people were killed in Sri Lanka; another 100,000 died along the other affected coasts. One of the victims was the 4 year old granddaughter of a good friend of theirs, Philippe, whom he had been babysitting as she played at the water's edge. Philippe watched her die as they were swept up by the wall of water, realizing that he, too, was perhaps unlikely to survive.

In his memoir, entitled *Lives Other Than My Own,* Carrere bears witness to the intense suffering and devastation that followed the tsunami. For days, he and his girlfriend and his sons helped recover bodies and tended to the grieving and wounded. Philippe did, in fact, survive, but then had to tell his daughter and her husband that young Juliette did not. Their broken hearts particularly touched Carrere, and together they enveloped Philippe's family with compassion and love and practical assistance. And it changed their lives. Carrere poignantly describes how a self-absorbed man such as himself can be changed by crisis and may, in fact, develop "a deep and perceptive capacity to see the struggles of others" in a new and profoundly empathic way. His heart had been opened by the losses and profound pain of others. His relationship with his partner subsequently grew and deepened in light of their shared heartache, and he came alive—becoming more loving—as never before.

The process of "opening up" and becoming more awake and aware is a complex and unpredictable one, but one that is often borne out of tragedy or suffering. The loss of a loved one, or of our security or of our health, can also mean the loss of our illusions, of our learned ways of making meaning, of our understanding of how things operate, of our beliefs and narrow perspectives. And with the expressed care and love of others, it can mark a new way of being or a profoundly redemptive experience.

I worked for many years as the chaplain on the heart transplant team at my medical center, during the early days of organ transplantation. Robert had just turned 65 years old and been forced to retire by a heart attack from a hard-driving, demanding career in business. He came in by ambulance, barely surviving an acute infarction as a result of blockage in his left descending artery, the one our doctors referred to as the widow-maker, which fed his left ventricle, the primary pumping chamber of his heart. He was slowly stabilized on full life support and maintained in the ICU on medications that supported his heart rhythm and his blood pressure, but he remained critically ill. With his heart muscle badly damaged, it quickly became clear that his only long-term option for survival would be a heart transplant, and only if a donor heart could be procured. The odds of that happening were long. Once he was weaned off the ventilator and could interact again without all the pain meds, I went with the cardiologist to tell Robert what had happened and what would be needed going forward. He was pragmatic and accepting, nodded his head, and said simply "Okay. Let's go!"

Over the next many days, I got to know Robert's wife, son, and daughter very well, while he hoped for the best. I learned from them that as he had been in his business, so was he in his family— demanding, emotionally distant, borderline abusive. Susan, his wife, told me that she had been considering leaving him until his first heart attack. The two adult kids, who stated they "loved him, but with reservations," had long felt somewhat alienated. But now, they were all present, rooting for him as best they could. For three weeks his future turned on getting a heart but, as fate would often have it, we were unable to find a donor who matched his blood type. Eventually, his kidney function began to deteriorate, which would disqualify for him for the transplant and result in his death, sooner rather than later. Again, I went into his room with the cardiologist, who informed him of his new reality and that he had been taken off the transplant list and that he wouldn't survive to leave the hospital. After the doctor left, Robert was silent for a long time, staring off into the distance, while I just sat by his side and waited. Eventually, he turned to me and asked, "So, this means I'm going to die, right?" I told him it did. "Soon?" "Likely," I responded, with a tender voice. Another period of silence ensued. And then, "Will you teach me how to do this?" As if.

Over the next three or four days, I had many interactions with Robert. He told me about his sorrows and his regrets, about how much he loved his wife and daughters and how he had never been able to show it, about how sad he was for how he had treated them, how determined he was to make things better. We actually scripted things he could say to them, as I haltingly tried to coach him toward opening his heart and speaking from his depths, telling them of his love for them, asking for their forgiveness, caring for them warmly and profoundly and fully. He responded tentatively, but then with courage and determination. When I got the page from his nurse a few days later that he was near death, I ran up to the room. As I looked in the window, I saw his wife and kids stroking his brow, holding his hands, embracing him gently and telling him they loved him. I was struck by the recognition that the entire ambience of the room had changed radically, as if filled with a kind of sacred warmth and peace. When he expired moments later, Susan saw me and came out of the room with a radiant, even serene look on her face. "I'm the most fortunate woman in the world," were her opening words to me. "I fell in love again with the young man I dated forty-five years ago. And I am so grateful. I know how much he loved me. I know how dearly he loved the kids. And he was so filled with love when he died. We'll all be okay."

Robert experienced a profound spiritual awakening in his final days. It wasn't about his religious beliefs or about his image of God. It was about his humanity, his recognition of his finitude, his resilience and resource-fulness. It was about opening his heart and authentically and powerfully expressing his deepest self, what he and I both came to understand was his true divine and loving nature.

Like so many others, Robert had not previously examined his way of being in the world, at least not openly or with anyone else. He hadn't sought input or guidance about how to express himself with any vulner-ability, about how to share his deep feelings, about how to disclose his self-doubts. Indeed, he initially had difficulty even identifying any feelings at all. And in that, as a hard-bitten, provider male, he was not unusual. He didn't have any kind of faith life or meditative practice, he wasn't in any kind of men's discussion group or therapy, and he was clueless about his own repressed spirituality. He had long confused his personal identity with his professional self and had acknowledged to me that for most of his life the only things that mattered were "climbing the ladder" and making as much money as possible. Like so many men in our distorted and divided culture, he lacked any sense of "interiority" or any expressions of grace in his primary relationships. And he had never been motivated to learn.

The opening of the heart is a natural process that, unfortunately, gets squashed early on for too many of us. We tend to only be able to do so—to open our hearts and develop deep awareness and spiritual intelli-gence—through years of learning, learning that requires *ongoing* input and reflection, dialogue and discussion, reading and study, perception and dis-cernment. Indeed, as Albert Einstein reportedly once said, "Once you stop learning, you start dying." And there are so many dynamics in modern life that tend to preclude the process. We medicate our emotional confusion and despair with alcohol and other drugs (many of which are prescribed), we blindly follow the guidance of charismatic figures instead of setting our own course, and we far too often resort to expressions of power and violence instead of seeking to understand and working to build common ground. We have come to realize that opening up is a choice that too many of us numbingly fail to make.

Training for a professional position in clinical spiritual care (pro-viding spiritual care in a clinical or hospital setting) required from me a certain spiritual intelligence, something that was difficult to articulate and hard to come by. I learned that it is something built upon a foundation of emotional maturity, self-understanding, and the ability to be clearly dif-ferentiated from others. I didn't start out with it, and I only opened up and developed those qualities over time, and then only in part. It came about slowly, through reflection on my experiences, through the teachings and feedback of my supervisors and mentors, through reading, and through the commitment to practice what I was learning, always being in a loop of reflection-amending-discovering-practicing. As I studied to become an educator in the field of clinical spiritual care, I continuously took on opportunities to make presentations, forcing me to study and prepare and integrate new learning. It was no different than standing in front of the mirror as a young seminary student, listening to Martin Luther King's sermons, and then trying to find a way to give them new expression. Spiritual intelligence requires a certain conscious commitment and intentionality to "make sense of things" and figure things out.

My work with students like Cheri and Jordan focused primarily on integrating their life stories and clarifying their boundaries, so that those stories and their growing awareness of "where they ended, and others began" would become resources for effective work with others. Learning to "lower our reactivity to the reactivity of others" would become an essential skill. Developing the capacity and freedom to move toward deep intimacy with a vulnerable stranger without losing perspective, was another.

Developing greater spiritual intelligence would require growing awareness of a broad range of theological and religious perspectives. It would require aligning that knowledge with a deepening understanding of psychology and therapeutic concepts. And it would mean synthesizing all of that with an appreciation of illness, trauma, crisis and the effects of medical treatment. How can anyone engage another person, to help them make sense of their reality and adapt to painful change, without deep sensitivity to what informs their feelings and their perspectives? That becomes especially true when those feelings are extreme, and when a person's perspectives are maladaptive or self-destructive. The training and education was always focused on opening up to new ways of being, on taking what they were learning and experiencing and making those learnings a core part of new self-expressions.

My students in the field of spiritual care had to develop clarity and depth around two key components: personal authority and professional identity. For the first, I had to learn how to confront my students' occasional dysfunctional and self-limiting thinking, in a gentle but direct manner, and then they, in turn, had to learn to do the same with their colleagues and patients. It was always about speaking the truth, but doing so in such a way as to empower the other to own that truth and want to make the change. Both my students and I saw that using the technique of figuratively "holding up a mirror" was powerfully effective. It was as if I was saying to them, "when you look in the mirror, can you see what I see?" And then I would prompt them to assess what they were seeing. How did they feel about what they were learning about themselves? And then finally, what to *do* about it: "Do you want to continue like that, or do you want to make a change?" Calling out inappropriate or insensitive or mindless behaviors became a key step for them in becoming more self-aware and spiritually intelligent, leading to the students themselves taking responsibility for their own and each other's learning.

For the second key element, professional identity, the concern was to help students become mindful of what they were truly wanting to be about. What did it mean for them, as spiritual care professionals in a complex medical setting, to *care* for another person? How did they want to be experienced? What was their purpose in going into a stranger's hospital room? How did they want to be perceived by their physician and nurse colleagues, by their patients' families and, for that matter, by their own families and friends? Slowly, they came to realize that their work was essentially to learn to be deeply empathic, reflective and generative, to prompt reflection in the patient, to facilitate adaptation to changing circumstances and to support the patient's own process of making meaning and quieting their own internal distress. It meant for the student learning to never tell a patient what they should think or do or believe, but always to be mindful to figure out how to raise the patient's consciousness and empower their own thoughts and actions. That in itself is a powerful distinction from the dominant culture of the evangelical church.

To become an effective spiritual care provider is to invite understanding and then adaptation, all as a pathway toward making decisions and interacting with loved ones in ways that are based on love rather than on anxiety or fear. It became a life lesson for so many. We gradually came to understand that not just our work, but our very lives were to be lived reflectively, with trust and courage, open to possibility and hope, and centered on justice, servanthood, and love. Both Cheri and Jordan made that adaptation, and it became freeing and empowering for them both. Over time, they opened up and embraced the reflective life, becoming first, effective professional care providers, and then successful leaders and teachers in their own right.

The same is true for all of us. To attain a meaningful level of spiritual intelligence is to—most importantly—be open to new input and new ways of being. It is to do our internal work, i.e., to work toward greater self-understanding and to learn to live as one who *initiates* rather than as one who primarily *reacts*. To open up is to explore the cumulative spiritual knowledge gleaned from the great religious movements down through human history in order to deepen our understanding of human behavior. To invite growth and depth is to embrace and understand the evolution and development of our species, of this world, of our universe. And it is to embrace mystery, opening our consciousness to movements of energy in and through our hearts and minds. Spiritual intelligence is about opening ourselves to what is often referred to as the Mind of God, or what I have come to recognize as the divine movement of the universal spirit in us and through us and around us, so that we become grounded, rooted and healthy.

Indeed, the human psyche is a complex and wondrous thing. How we make sense out of our circumstances, how we adapt to change, how we choose to express ourselves and live in relationship, how we shape our values and ideals, how we respond to trauma, how we discern the sacred, how we *thrive* . . . , such are the things that make life fascinating and wondrous, if also painful and challenging.

Making sense out of things is a process that perhaps has never been more important than currently. I am writing during poignant and powerful days in the US and around the world. We are wrestling with the hundreds of thousands of American lives lost from the coronavirus pandemic—even as it wound down, only to rise up again with the Delta variant—recognizing, too, how our social fabric has been stretched and threatened. We are wrestling with ongoing resistance to taking the vaccine and with the voices on far right news channels encouraging the resistance, in spite of continuing and increasing risks. We are wrestling with autocratic political leaders fueling deepening political and social divisions, both nationally and internationally. The rise of conspiracy theories, fed by the social networks and by promises of the instant gratification of anonymous power, have created extremist on-line communities and raised the specter of social violence. The forced isolation of the last nearly two years, together with the economic shifts and resulting inflation, are challenging our resourcefulness and our resilience in ways my generation has not previously experienced.

Confusion and unease abound. All these issues and concerns may or may not resolve soon; still, their effects will be in our psyches for a long time.

Even more importantly perhaps, we are on the cusp of multiple global crises. Climate change is wreaking havoc on coastal areas and farmlands around the world. The extinction rate of diverse species of both plants and animals in increasing. Global hunger and poverty and migration are once again on the rise. Addictions, emotional illness, domestic abuse, suicides— all are trending upward. As fear generalizes, we polarize and retrench, giving rise to adversarial behaviors, the proliferation of firearms, conspiracy theories, autocratic politicians and expressions of nationalism and racism, and on and on. How, then, shall we live?

I take courage, however, that where there is decline, there is rebirth as well, and the current rising up of new ways of thinking and being is encouraging and hopeful. The *Me Too* and *Black Lives Matter* movements have generated tremendous energy to seek true structural change and greater social and economic justice and equity. The money being poured into infrastructure is giving renewed hope to the economically marginalized. The efforts to prioritize climate change and gun control are being energized by an emerging generation of young people who are passionately motivated. The distortions in American religion are receiving greater scrutiny than ever, augmented by a groundswell of interest in all things spiritual, as we search for something new and more deeply meaningful. The widespread distress and feelings of alienation experienced by so many are being balanced by an explosion of spirit arising within the collective psyche of humanity. A quiet candlelight of hope is glimmering in the darkness and generating new engagement with the human condition. As difficult as these days are, so are they filled with huge potential. Indeed, realizing that potential may turn on each one of us giving voice to what is rising up within.

Chapter Six

Existential Suffering & Making Meaning

"The Bushmen in the Kalahari Desert talk about the two 'hungers'. There is the Great Hunger and there is the Little Hunger. The Little Hunger wants food for the belly; but the Great Hunger, the greatest hunger of all, is the hunger for meaning . . . Once what you are doing has for you meaning, it is irrelevant whether you are happy or unhappy. You are content—you are not alone in your spirit—you belong."

—LAURENS VAN DER POST, *THE HEART OF THE HUNTER*

IT HAS BECOME INCREASINGLY clear that we have crossed the *postmodern* divide in our culture, where truth is relative, where distrust trumps personal benefit, and where the status quo gets conflated with personal security. This is true across the board, in religion, in business, in politics, and maybe most especially in healthcare. We have moved from the *modern* experience of health care, where we were promised deliverance through technical expertise and complex organizations of treatment for *all* our people, to a postmodern experience, where the potential for healing has been unwittingly accompanied by a loss of voice, perspective, and meaning, most especially for the marginalized. And the percentage of those marginalized, by being unable to access insurance and healthcare at reasonable cost, is growing once again in the US, a true national disgrace.

Loss of autonomy and choice and meaning may be most profound for us at the end of life. Being cared for by strangers as we come toward the end of life can be not only inefficient, but ultimately dehumanizing. Alongside our remarkable and growing capacity to intervene into aging and illness, we have also disembodied it. How often did I see my colleagues and I get caught in the dilemma of working diligently and faithfully to prolong life only to witness abject suffering; of seeking restoration of the body only to witness the splitting off of the spirit; of valiantly struggling to stave off death only to generate despair and isolation? In postmodernism, the illusion of our ability to hold off death open-endedly unwittingly supports forgetting that death is a part of the human condition.

Our fear of death has led to a massive assault on it. Consequently, driven by cultural expectations, we crave virtually any life-prolonging technology. More than ever, we feel morally compelled to prolong life—virtually any form of life—as long as possible. Advanced healthcare directives still are not widely used, and when they are, they are still over-ridden a significant percent of the time. When we were first learning that the coronavirus pandemic was going to expand exponentially and be devastating for older folk and persons with comorbidities, our government prioritized the manufacture and distribution of ventilators over vaccinations and pharmaceutical treatments, even though the likelihood of survival on the ventilator for Covid patients was extremely low. This orientation is in keeping with the commonly-held construct in contemporary medical culture that "the best death is the one that can be put off the longest." But human experience at the end of life in our current system is teaching a deeper lesson. The struggle of our patients to find meaning in the face of our compulsive efforts to defeat death becomes—paradoxically—life denying. Too often, we leave our patients alone to work through the inherent dilemmas, abdicating our role as healers. And the dehumanization of the patient, in turn, tends to dehumanize the care provider as well.

We, as a nation, have taken a significant step forward in recent years, establishing Palliative Care teams and hospice programs, and providing consultation and support services to primary physicians and their patients who are dying. Clearly, creative, advanced care planning and bereavement support are important components of the efforts to transform our work with the progressively, chronically ill. Empowering such people to make self-affirming, sacred, and dignified choices about how and where they will die is a first step to giving voice and making sense once again of life and death in these postmodern times. But, in truth, such resources are often accessed late, and too many of us face our finitude fearfully, silently, and alone. The costs, both financial and personal, are high and the economic divide only exacerbates the problem.

It has been interesting to note that Palliative Care teams see Spiritual Care (a chaplain) as an essential component of the team. Studies have shown that when a skilled chaplain is able to reflect honestly and openly with patients and family members, both 'hospital days' and healthcare costs decrease, even as patient satisfaction goes up. But given the pandemic, and halting conversations happening only by phone, the effort to shape meaning and self-affirming decision-making has too-often faltered. Effective palliative care, and meaningful end-of-life care, requires close, intimate and reflective conversations. When patients feel supported, heard and cared about, death itself takes on a gently different quality.

One of the tasks before us, as we become more spiritually intelligent, is to bring death itself back into a human scale. We need to re-imagine dying and reflect together about ways to do this. We know well in theory how to provide care and even improve living when cure is unlikely; the harder task is to create the social dialogue and implement the nuanced changes required. Theology and medicine cannot absent themselves from this conversation. The almost single-minded focus on decision-making that has infused our conversations may only divert attention from what is most significantly needed—the moral courage to acknowledge limits and mortality. Contemporary religion has not yet taken on the task of speaking thoughtfully and reflectively about dying, and the challenge is to do so not only with medical sophistication but also with deep compassion and care for the human experience. Simply put, it is hard to reframe the dialogue when death remains a deeply feared enemy.

With all that is available to us, perhaps the most important resource we have is ourselves. If we, as thoughtful and sensitive human beings, can recover our humility before the awesome moments of death and learn to truly *be* with each other—one human being to another—we might be able to embrace the reality that death is not always open to solutions and that we can transform it only by finding meaning in it. And that is primarily a spiritual process, informed by trust and acceptance and, ultimately, faith. In doing so, we might be able to quiet the psychic fears, and increase the convictions of being in the care of the divine mysteries in such a way that acceptance of our finitude and of our inevitable dying becomes the norm.

Facile statements about God and rote prayers leave many of us wanting. Rather, embracing the divine mysteries and the unknown, and then discerning the sense of being borne up by a heritage of enduring love and acceptance, seems to be what quiets the soul. Is that not a key to becoming spiritually intelligent, to trusting the unfolding, to loving ourselves and each other through the aging and vulnerability and eventual separation?

One way to get at shifting the cultural conversation is to reflect on what we might refer to as existential suffering—the suffering of the soul that is rooted in the loss of meaning. It is a topic I am somewhat reluctant to write about, simply because it is a difficult issue to even attempt to capture, to discuss rationally and cogently. I have come to appreciate the term "the unspeakable darkness" following so many long conversations with hundreds of dying patients, and with dozens of patients caught in deep mental illness, such as schizophrenia and profound depression. The term comes in fact, from Arthur Frank, one of my favorite authors. He wrote powerfully about how the reflective qualities associated with extreme suffering—hopelessness, meaninglessness, remorse, anxiety, etc.—give way to something deeper, something un-nameable, often something that can only be captured through poetry, art and the metaphoric language of religious texts. Sometimes people who experience deep suffering fall into silence, but respond to music and poetry and art with tears in their eyes.

I will always remember the nineteen-year-old African American kid from the inner city, very much into the hip-hop culture, but now struggling with a new diagnosis of drug abuse-induced cardiomyopathy, with a long-odds transplant being his only hope for survival. His whole world had come to a screeching halt. He wasn't very articulate, he was scared to death, and he didn't trust anyone, understandably. But he could draw. And my goodness the pain he poured into his pictures, graphic, violent, despairing, I'll never forget them. When Amanda Gorman gave her poetic and moving reading at the 2021 Presidential Inauguration, I had tears in my eyes because I recognized the existential suffering out of which her words were borne.

At the same time, I am nonetheless encouraged to reflect about existential suffering, because it is something we all understand at least in part, something we all share and have thoughts and feelings about, and if ever there was a topic to capture the deep shadow-side essence of the human condition, this is it. We all, on some level, understand what it is to suffer unimaginably, to experience painful, unbearable, insults to the body and psyche. And even if we ourselves haven't yet experienced such crises, we can all envision what it will be like when our turn does come, because we've certainly seen it in our loved ones. And if you've worked with the devastating dynamics of progressive illness and seen its effects, or with spinal cord injury patients, or with survivors of their spouse's sudden death, or with the despair that leads to a loss of hope and the slow slide into mental illness or homelessness or suicidal ideation, then you know that rarely does a day go by that we don't encounter deep suffering in others, standing often as silent witnesses to the pain and brokenness of human life. It is not an easy thing.

I might go so far as to say that existential suffering—suffering that is so painful that we lose all sense of grounding, all sense of meaning, all sense of otherness and connection and future—is something we all know or will know, in some form, personally. Ask anyone of any age, and they will tell you they "know." They perceive it and feel it, out there, just on the edge of consciousness somewhere, held at bay for as long as possible by our denial and rationalization. Indeed, suffering is, in part, what defines us as human, as reflective, thoughtful, *compassionate* beings.

Robert Cantwell was a child oncologist at Minneapolis Children's Medical Center during my residency in clinical spiritual care in 1985. He was an intimidating figure, tall, broad-shouldered, good-looking, only his late forties; he seemingly had everything going for him. And he was kind but somewhat remote, dynamic but a bit austere. He was an excellent doc, and someone I really admired, in part because he was deeply moved by the plight of the kids for whom he was caring. He would pull me in on most cases, telling the parents that he would like them to talk with me. And that way he could contain his feelings and maintain his demeanor and avoid the vulnerable intimacy that our work so requires. I understood his need to protect himself, even though I suspect he wasn't very conscious of what he was doing. We'd gotten to know each other pretty well around the deaths of a couple of the most vulnerable of our patients and, in part, because he attended a couple of the funerals that I did that year.

But then came that day when he grabbed me by the shirt sleeve and asked me to come with him back to his office. And without anything to soften it, he told me that he himself had just been diagnosed with a debilitating, life-threatening illness, and if I remember right, it was primary liver cancer, a relatively rare illness in an otherwise healthy man. It had hit him out of the blue. And this was back when cancer was a contraindication to liver transplantation, and there just would be no hopeful treatment options available to him.

And how painful. He fought hard to maintain composure, and then stated very simply and humbly, "I need you to be my chaplain." And over the next several weeks, he expressed to me, haltingly, the rending of his soul, the abject brokenness that he was experiencing. There was no comforting him. There would be no reframing, no making sense of, no letting go. His professional world—and his whole life as he knew it—had ended with his diagnosis. He didn't have children of his own, and he didn't have a religious faith. He had been professionally trained without attention being paid to the spiritual, and the fraternity of medicine was his whole universe, having placed his entire faith in his ability to bring to bear the best that science had to offer. He wasn't angry about his prognosis, but he was deeply despairing, pouring out his angst and inability to understand, deeply lamenting, desperately searching for alternative cures, but then gradually becoming silent, his remoteness inevitably and slowly just taking over. It was existential suffering of the first order. And when he died, it was one of the saddest experiences of my career, because I had come to care deeply for him, and because I couldn't help him, I couldn't break through the meaninglessness. He taught me a lot about dignity, but unfortunately, a lot about true despair as well, suffering silently, enduring his decline stoically, withdrawing in the end into total isolation. Never again would I be facile about dying, or about how I would work with someone experiencing it.

By contrast I also want to relay the story of Noreen, who died recently. Noreen was a student of mine in the mid 90's. She became a pastor in a large and wealthy suburban congregation, an author and a teacher and a wonderfully progressive voice, an all-around wise woman. And I loved her dearly. When she first called me, three and half years earlier, to come meet her in her office at the church, I had no idea that she would tell me that she had been diagnosed the day before with non-small cell carcinoma of the lung, stage 3, inoperable. And then, in response to my inquiry about what that meant for her, she stated simply, "It means I am dying." And indeed, that's exactly what it meant. The docs had estimated six to twelve months life expectancy, but she lived mostly well and fully for two-plus years, until just three weeks before her death. We met for coffee and conversation once a month throughout her illness, I was a first-hand witness to her suffering that resulted from the side effects of her treatment—the backing up of her IV chemo into her arm causing extreme pain and tissue erosion and loss of its use for six months, the leeching out of a new and especially toxic chemo from the bottoms of her feet, burning her soles and hobbling her ability to walk, the multiple bouts with nausea and migraines and hair loss and weight loss. But it just never dampened her spirits. After our initial time together, during which we both wept pretty freely, laughter and love became her primary ways of being. When she would have periods of relative health and recovery, she wouldn't let people deny her reality, always and consistently reminding people that she was dying, but then smiling and saying that she was also living, more fully than ever. She made her bucket list, and did most everything on it, taking her kids to Europe, going away on romantic holidays with her husband, skydiving, not just once but again on the anniversary of the first one. Skiing up at Whistler and scuba diving in Hawaii. And preaching whenever she could muster the energy, always holding down at least a ten percent position at the church.

Noreen taught me how to die well and how to go out with gratitude, refusing to get caught up in the pain or the sorrow of leaving. When she finally went into hospice care at home, she had a party to celebrate beating the odds for so long. She was surrounded by loving family and friends. She was suffering, but it was not existential. Indeed, she said, she had never felt closer to the divine spirit, or more alive than when she was dying. The last time I talked with her on the phone, slurring her words a bit from all the pain meds and struggling to concentrate, she told me the lift mechanism used to get her from the bed to a standing position made her feel like a star in the Cirque d'Soleil! And a star she truly was. Remarkable.

I tell you about both of these significant teachers in my life to tune us in to how we learn and how we become more spiritually intelligent and begin to make meaning in life. Our friends and loved ones and colleagues and patients open our hearts and deepen our compassion, if only we listen closely. As if provided from an external source, we find the wherewithal to be truly present. It requires reflection and contemplation, that quality of patience and focus required to look at something for a long time and allow our minds to take it in and inform new perspectives. I love how Joan Chittister put it:

> *Contemplation is a very dangerous activity. It not only brings us face to face with God. It brings us, as well, face to face with the world, face to face with the self. And then, of course, something must be done. Nothing stays the same once we have found the God within . . . . We carry the world in our hearts: the oppression of all peoples,*

the suffering of our friends, the burdens of our enemies, the raping of
the Earth, the hunger of the starving, the joy of every laughing child.[1]

I am mindful of the beautiful and painful reflections by a writer and mystic known as St. John of the Cross in the late 1500s. He was writing in Spain during the horrific years of the Counter Reformation, and is best known as the one who wrote about existential suffering as the "long dark night of the soul."[2] John's father had died when he was only three, and then his brother a couple years later, from the poverty and malnutrition to which they had been reduced. Nonetheless, he endured, surviving an orphanage, committing to an education, eventually becoming a priest and a reformer. But then he was imprisoned by the ruling class of the Church for his re-forming work, where he was isolated and tortured. Still, he endured, eventually going on to establish convents and to teach and write. And today, the Catholic Church venerates him as a saint. His legacy became his witness to how he saw such profoundly painful suffering not only as something to be endured but also to be, somehow, embraced, as a time for deep contemplation, reflecting on it in the light of what shaped meaning in his life, which for him was the gospel of Jesus. Indeed, he saw such contemplation as the key process for coming to acceptance and for beginning to make meaning, for refining a new pathway for reconnecting to the divine spirit. His witness was both simple and profound: that in the midst of suffering and isolation, we experience the potential for a deeper connection with the divine spirit, for a soul-transforming recognition of true transcendence.

Though I hope not to that extreme, you and I can appreciate what it is to endure a long, dark night of the soul, when "all else is gone." Such suffering reshapes our lives, and if it doesn't break us, we end up, potentially, re-oriented, re-made. We never see things the same way again. The fear of dying recedes, replaced by an abiding trust of being borne-up by the divine, come what may. We recognize and begin to feel with the pain of others and the pain of the world. To embrace such a re-orientation is to begin to heal, if only in part, and to begin anew to live a more meaningful life, to become spiritually attuned and aware and alive.

In my doctoral program, I took one course on Christian Ethics from a brilliant, if somewhat austere, professor. I came to appreciate him greatly, however, over the course of our readings and dialogues, and I was always struck by his matter-of-factness, and by his equanimity. He was

1. Chittister and Rohr, *Prophets Then, Prophets Now,* Audio CD 1/1/2006
2. St. John of the Cross, *Dark Night of the Soul*

post-retirement age at the time, in his early-70s, but he loved still to teach on occasion, and I was grateful for him. A couple years after I completed the course, I heard from a friend that his knee had given out on him coming in the back door of his house, and he stumbled, falling down the basement stairs. It must have been a horrific fall. I called a colleague at the hospital that was caring for him, and was told he had suffered a high spinal fracture, was paralyzed, and would be unlikely to get any meaningful recovery or independence again. I felt deep sadness, sent him a card, and did my best to empathize. But a couple of weeks later, I got word that he was being transferred to my hospital for assessment and potential rehabilitation, now that his ventilator had been removed and he was able to breathe on his own. I was momentarily heartened. But then I got a phone call from his wife, asking if I would meet with them once they were settled in, and she told me then that the injuries were "devastating," I think, primarily, to prepare me. And indeed, it was difficult to absorb. He was strapped in a mechanical chair, tipped way back, with his head, legs and wrists all restrained to manage the involuntary spasms. He couldn't move anything intentionally. He had a mirror arranged above his eyes so he could see whoever came to talk with him, but his voice was weak, and his eyes were usually closed. It was impossible to figure out how to connect with him. I talked with his physician who told me his potential for recovering any movement in his arms was very low, and that he just didn't know if he could recover enough to even get home.

The second day I went to see him, they tipped up his chair enough that we could look directly at each other. After a few uncomfortable minutes of trying to find ways to express ourselves meaningfully to each other, I asked him "what he needed." He raised an eyebrow, and looked at me for a long time. Then his wife pulled in close and put her hand on his cheek. It was clear to me they had been talking. And then he said to me, slowly and painfully, "I need—I want—to go home. I want to sit in the warmth of my sunroom, and have a glass of wine with my wife. And then I want to be put in my bed and have the hospice people make me comfortable, and then let me sleep away." "I can make that happen," I said. We both knew fully well what that meant. "If you would help me with that, I would be eternally grateful," he whispered. And then to his wife, "It's okay. I have no fear of dying. My life, as you know, really ended three weeks ago. This is what I want." And she nodded, and wept, and we held each other. Two days later, his desire was fulfilled, and his death came gracefully.

❀❀❀❀❀

And so, we can self-describe as concerned with all of human suffering, and as wounded healers ourselves. Henri Nouwen's wonderful book, *The Wounded Healer*, was relatively small and not anticipated to have a major impact. No one was more surprised by the buzz it created in the field of spiritual care than Henri Nouwen himself. He had written it as a very personal reflection, as a matter of the heart and soul, as an attempt to capture the essence of the work that was so often poorly done if only because the people who were providing it, the pastors and priests and nuns and traditional hospital chaplains, were, in his experience, unconsciously self-protective, bent on maintaining critical objectivity.

Nouwen called all practitioners of spiritual care into the intimate encounter, that is, into the depths of very subjective soul work, and key to the process of moving into intimacy with another was to become contemplative and—specifically—to embrace one's own woundedness. How could any of us be true healers, until we could work through our own existential struggles and face our own mortality directly, being able to access it in fact, as a resource for meaningful spiritual care? That book turned our whole profession around, and opened the doors for it to become a true clinical discipline. Our training methods changed significantly after that, as our own feelings, reflections and personal processes of integration became a part of the curriculum. And his point was simple: we can all speak with wisdom, because we all know the pain of losing our grounding, the first true criteria of existential suffering.

So, let's try to break it down a little, and get inside the question of what makes existential suffering "existential?" In this regard, I suggest there are three broad ways of thinking about it. Most of the literature states that suffering becomes qualitatively different, significantly more painful, when one is confronted by the reality of their own dying. Getting a terminal diagnosis changes things, and is generally a precondition of talking about existential suffering. All the protective layers of the psyche drop away, and the exposure to a terrifying new reality is pretty raw. And honestly, most of us haven't integrated our personal theologies enough (our ways of making sense out of how the world and the divine spirit works, our ways of maintaining a sense of personal security) to retain *any* quality of equanimity.

Countless times I have been with people on the front end of such news. When Richard, 62 years old and having just been elevated to a senior position in his company, came into the hospital with a heart attack, only to discover he had an aggressive and terminal lymphoma as well, I just watched his eyes. He looked at me for the longest time, never breaking eye contact, and I saw pretty much every emotion imaginable pass through them, until finally, the fear took over and he began to shake and tremble, having trouble breathing. That too, was a powerfully intimate moment, leading to him asking me to help him, which I indeed tried to do, by hook or by crook as my grandma used to say. Richard, too, was one of my teachers, as he navigated through his powerfully existential experience of suffering.

But it certainly doesn't apply only to the dying. It also applies to those caught up in the helplessness of accompanying the dying or experiencing sudden and unexpected loss—the spouse or partner or child. One of my closest friends grew up in a small town on the prairie of North Dakota, where life was pretty idyllic and secure. When he was a teenager, his world was shattered by the deaths of his parents a year apart, both from cancer. Brian and his brother were taken in by the neighbor family across the street, who tended to them as their own, provided for them through high school, gave them unqualified and unconditional love and support, and helped them both select a college, where my relationship with Brian began. He was a resilient and wonderful guy, but he also carried within him a deep sorrow, notable only to those of us closest to him. He married his college sweetheart, and we decided together to both go to the seminary. Pauline, his wife, was a kindred spirit to Brian, and she was beautiful, in both body and soul. So, when she, in turn, became ill with Primary Pulmonary Hypertension, it seemed somehow totally, nightmarishly wrong. And it progressed rapidly. Brian was serving as the pastor at a small Lutheran church in California when she was admitted to Stanford University Medical Center, where she eventually died in Brian's arms. When he called me to tell me about it, he was inconsolable. His despair was total. He stated very simply, "I don't think I can survive this." Indeed. And it took a long time, a time filled with deep grief, contemplation, reflection, struggle and prayer. Today, he is a witness to beginning life anew after a devastating loss. After a fruitful and wonderful career in ministry, Brian recently retired from serving a large church in Washington DC. He had married again—they had two beautiful kids who are now thriving adults—and is contentedly doing writing and teaching, a testament to his spiritual depth and resilience.

A third broad way of thinking about existential suffering has to do with getting caught up in violent trauma, and here is where I want to reference one of the severe costs of war on the soul. Another dear friend, Howard, retired as the Chief of Chaplains of the Air Force, a Major General. In the early nineties, he was deployed as a chaplain with the 363rd Tactical Fighter Wing and sent to the first Gulf war. And on one of those awful days at Al Dhafra Air Base in the United Arab Emirates—a classified location from which the Air Force flew missions into Iraq—two air crew members got hit over the gulf and did not return, crashing back into the desert just a few miles from base. Howard was a part of the crash recovery team that went out to recover the bodies, and then had to provide the memorial service. He wrote me a profoundly moving letter, in which he poured out his horror and sorrow and existential struggle, wondering if he, too, could go on professionally to do more of the work required.

I know that Howard personally tended to dozens if not hundreds of deaths over the years, and tended to even more airmen who were struggling with post-traumatic stress, always experiencing their pain, never losing heart. When serving at the Pentagon, he would on occasion receive wounded military personnel as guests at the Pentagon or visit gravely injured airmen who had lost limbs or suffered severe cognitive insults and were now receiving treatment at Walter Reed National Military Medical Center. One of the great tragedies of that conflict and the resulting long-term wars in Iraq and Afghanistan is the large number of military members who have had to wrestle so deeply with PTSD. The research in PTSD, by the way, gives a profound insight to existential suffering. Witnessing horrific events and being exposed to sudden and violent images, including the potential of your own death, is tremendously difficult to integrate. Yet, more even than witnessing or experiencing trauma, the thing that appears hardest for military members to fit into their meaning frameworks, and therefore to adapt to in healthy ways, is actually participating in the violence themselves, going against their own moral code, if you will. Existential suffering can have to do with a deep sense of guilt and shame, even as they rationally know it needed to happen. War devastates the human spirit in so many ways and on so many levels. Because he understood that, Howard's expressions of care were profoundly appreciated by hundreds of them, wounded in both body and spirit.

We might think about existential suffering as that kind of suffering that is primarily known by the experience of the loss of "grounded-ness," of becoming ground*less*. One of my patients referred to it as akin to being pushed out of an airplane without a parachute. It references those experiences that devastate, where the rug gets swept away completely, where the event is so profoundly shattering that we feel lost and completely un-moored. The author Sally Anderson, in a profound personal account of tragedy and loss and eventual recovery, entitled Free Fall, broke it down this way: the sense of groundlessness is reflective of being *shaken to the core* where "a crack appears in our carefully crafted concept of reality and where the very nature of reality is experienced in a new, terrifying way. We are sucked into the startling realization that the rules of the game are not what we imagined them to be."[3] It is a time of raw experience and frayed emotions, of discontinuity, pain, despair, abject sorrow and anger. And it is a time of feeling lost, isolated, alienated from the world and perhaps most especially, alienated from God, where *nothing* comforts and *nothing* makes sense; where, in fact, we have an experience of abject hopelessness.

Consider for a moment the personal videos at the Holocaust Museum in Washington D.C. In the last exhibit, you sit in front of video screens in a very small, open amphitheater, totally engaged in the powerful and painful recollections. Person after person, survivor after survivor, tell what they experienced, bearing witness to the unspeakable, noting the paralysis. In some of them, those telling their stories used "un" terms to try to capture the experience of losing grounded-ness: un-raveled, un-done, un-hinged, un-able to reconcile their experience with their spiritual faith, having their beliefs "shattered," experiencing "extreme dissonance" in their way of mak-ing sense of things, becoming emotionally paralyzed. One of the threads in the writings of Holocaust survivors, as a matter of fact, is that that sense of being paralyzed was universal, a true response of the human psyche to extreme violation and violence. It was a direct result of the extreme horror, of not being able to make sense of what was happening, of the shock and disbelief, and then of the free fall through the quick loss of grounding—the despair and helplessness and sense of all things coming undone, all things held dear being taken. And that experience paralyzes people. It is the psy-chology of genocide and mass slaughter, by the way, and it has much to teach us about the experience of existential suffering in ourselves and in critically ill patients.

No one gets through that exhibit without coming to a profound ap-preciation of existential suffering. It is an experience of horror, deep sorrow, profound angst, tears, helplessness, muted expressions. The paralysis gets felt deeply and personally, and it demonstrates how such horror becomes soul-shattering. And they tell their stories and bear their witness in order

---

3. Anderson, *Free Fall*, 29.

to continue their recovery and to get past for all time that initial paralysis, not just of each individual, but of the Jewish people, of society as a whole. Courage—the resolve to never again accept such a fate combined with re-dedicated efforts to building understanding and cooperation—is the beginning to reclaim one's ground.

Paul Tillich, in his book *The Courage To Be*, was the first to write about the experience of, or *condition* of, what he called "non-being."[4] Becoming groundless has a sense of complete lost-ness, of abandonment, of no longer having any sense of divine validation as worthy or worthwhile, of no longer having any sense of value, of no longer having any "being," of becoming indifferent to life itself. I've only encountered it a few times in my career, but it has been pretty haunting when I have. I remember one younger person in particular. He was an adolescent who had not matured or evolved to a place of being able to keep perspective on his illness. He, too, was waiting for a heart transplant, on powerful medications to support his blood pressure, his heart barely pumping, unable to get out of bed, alienated from his parents. And day after day he lingered and just slowly withdrew, "curved inward" to use another of Tillich's phrases, keeping his room dark, refusing to talk to anyone, having little or no sense of self left. I remember our cardiologist saying to me one day after coming out of his room, *"If we lose this kid to depression, I am putting it on you. Don't you dare let him die from losing the will to live!"*

Well, that did indeed put it to me. It was at the point where any emotion, any expression, would have been better than none, so I went into the room that afternoon, threw open the curtains, turned on the lights, and prepared to endure his wrath. But he was silent, staring, seemingly not even hearing, almost catatonic, literally dying in front of me, or so it seemed. We got him back, but it took all of us, supporting, confronting, accompanying, encouraging, challenging him, contracting with him, until he finally received a donor heart, and the last I knew he was making it in the larger world, and going to college, but it was an experience I will never forget, as close to a situation of emotional death causing physical death as I would ever want to see.

For older, more mature adults, the literature suggests that the other primary expression in the face of groundlessness is the desire to just be at peace. For some, that means letting death come, and just getting it over with. For others, it means lowering the bar, from a hoped for experience of

---

4. Tillich, *The Courage To Be*, 90.

deliverance to settling for anything that will just quiet the suffering for a little while, some way to make their condition more manageable, more stable. Clarice was a patient of mine who had had multiple surgeries in her twenties for extreme Crohn's disease and upper GI inflammation. Something had happened during surgery, a nerve got damaged, or a neural pathway got lit up somehow, and she was forced to live with constant and occasionally intense pain. She worked hard with the medical team to find the right combinations of pain medication that would dull her pain without dulling her life, wanting desperately to be able to raise her son and continue a career that had been so suddenly interrupted. She had hoped for and fought for a resolution to her pain, but never successfully and now, a couple years later, the docs were beginning to tire of her, and she was getting labeled as drug-seeking, and she asked if I might help her. Her cry and her prayer was now nothing more than finding a middle ground, some stability, a sense of making peace with what she had come to refer to as her constant painful companion. She is still making it today, in chronic pain, living one day at a time, one hour at a time. I occasionally invited her into my student groups, to sensitize them to working with people in significant pain, and she was a wonderful teacher.

The longing for grounding is enacted in four overlapping ways, two that are self-limiting and two that, on the other hand, are life-enhancing. On the negative side, the research (and our own personal experiences, I might add) suggests that people who are caught in existential suffering and who are seeking to get grounded once again either tend to suppress their thoughts and refuse to think about or process it, or they get caught up in their despondency and sense of victimization. We all have experienced both many times over. As a chaplain, I made my living by moving into the intimate reflective spaces with patients in an effort to make meaning and to facilitate adaptation to changing circumstances in healthy ways. So, I was always struck by those who just didn't want to talk about things, or who didn't want any messages that reflected an uncomfortable reality, or who just wanted to conscript me into supporting their denial (not something I tended to do). But I understood it was a natural defense against the meaninglessness of existential pain. "Let's just avoid it, or I will break down or become suicidal or whatever," was the unspoken message. I teach my students and clients today to recognize silence as a defense mechanism that is indicative of and proportionate to the suffering, and therefore needs to be engaged, sensitively and compassionately; it is the patient's way of trying to get grounded once again, inadequate though it may be.

And then there are those who get caught in their anger and resentment and despondency: angry perhaps at the divine or at life or at circumstances, resentful of their fate, wrapping themselves up in the question of "Why me?" These are the patients chaplains tend to tire of quickly, not wanting to work with their complaining, not willing to stay present and do the hard work of engaging and reframing (more about that in a moment). They also tend to be the patients who never fully individuated, who tend toward the shame-based side of the spectrum, who orient toward life with wariness and self-protection and felt inadequacy. I actually liked working with these patients because I could identify with them, and because, if I could find the right moment and the vulnerable issue, they were so often hungry to learn and grow.

The more positive ways in which ill or traumatized people tend to enact their longing for grounding are by turning into the discomfort and engaging their new reality, and by choosing to live in the in-between of embracing what they can and making space for what they don't yet understand. Note that here I am turning toward the process of trying to shine a glimmer of light into their unspeakable darkness.

For such people to become spiritually intelligent and emotionally resourceful, they need, with help, to turn *toward* the discomfort, in an effort to explore it, understand it, make sense of it, and find meaning in it. Most will do that on their own, if slowly or irregularly or in fits and starts. It is all a part of trying to re-establish grounding, which is very much a universal human trait. We might say that the soul *seeks* health. And this primarily has to do with "finding one's place in the world" and settling that sense of disconnection. In my experience, this is where the god question really gets engaged: trying to understand—in light of what has happened—who or what "God" is (and here I mean the God of many names or of no name—all of humankind's efforts to conceptualize the holy other), what God does, and how to relate to God in this new reality.

It has been interesting to note that for most people caught in existential suffering, their previous understandings of the divine spirit, and of life itself, are simply inadequate. And I've become something of a critic of the church and organized religion as a result of my engagement with these issues. Rarely do I find ministers addressing the existential questions and the great mysteries of life in an evolving universe, tending instead to promote and protect the traditional perspectives of scripture-based interpretations. The big questions, for which there are no definitive answers, tend to get relegated to private conversations. And what has been true for me is also true for everyone. Even people who have been deeply involved in the communities of their religious faith often come up wanting when facing an existential crisis; they find too often that what they have been taught and what they have held to, in terms of their religious beliefs, is less than adequate to speak to current life circumstances.

That certainly isn't true for everyone, but it is for many. I remember one wonderful exception, another one of my teachers, an older woman dying in the coronary care unit in which I was working, who had spent her whole life on the farm in southwestern Minnesota. Life and death, struggle and hard work, community and family—they defined her daily experience and shaped her meaning-making. Cows, hogs, horses, chickens . . . ; she lived deeply in the rhythm of being born and dying; she knew the exigencies of nature, the storms and the calm, the sun and the rain; she loved detasseling the corn every August, and "walking the beans" in the spring (that's pulling up the stray corn shoots in the soybean fields, if you're not familiar with farming), and harvesting the squash and apples in the fall, and she trusted the turning of the seasons, quoting to me, in fact, the famous passage from Ecclesiastes. She had no questions about her dying, and her trust in her God was complete, fully supported by her years of Sunday worship and family gatherings in the church that had served her community for generations. In her mind she was strongly grounded in the belief that she would soon be with her husband and her son who had died as an infant and all the saints that went before her and who had been, as she stated, referencing the Pauline passage, "cheering her on" as she faithfully did her tasks and embraced her life on the land. She was an earthy, centered woman. And she was content that her other children would carry on her legacy and take good care of the land she loved, good stewards of God's gifts, solid, loving, grounded. She was a wonderful woman. And she knew that life was fragile and temporary, and that she could die at any time. And it was well with her soul.

But it has been my experience that most of us raised in contemporary society have had to struggle it through in less secure ways. And it all turns on letting go, including letting go of the 'too narrow' god images that we have held to previously, and on changing our understanding of how the divine spirit works in the world. The distant sky God—the authoritarian capricious God of patriarchy, the God we strangely assume who has a plan for our lives, the God of our childhood beliefs—no longer works for most people who suffer, primarily because it tends to feel remote, immutable, even futile, contributing to the cycles of blame, anger, resentment and victimization. To make the shift toward a spirituality that is life-giving and generative, most people reconfigure their understanding of the divine spirit toward one that is compassionately present, who changes hearts and minds through loving engagement but who doesn't or can't intervene directly in things to change outcomes. Prayer gets refocused around lowering our self-protective and unconscious filters in order to better experience the movement of the divine spirit all around us and even within us, rather than on asking for deliverance. And trust begins to become a core essential, giving rise to the recognition of ongoing creation, re-creation, healing and renewal—continual processes that we participate *in*, rather than look to have miraculously provided. We *turn toward* the discomfort (I actually like the concept of *leaning into* the discomfort) and we learn to embrace the free fall, trusting that we will indeed be borne up, come what may, that we will ever be in the mysterious care of the divine—a mystery that perhaps from this vantage point we are just simply unable to envision or fully comprehend.

❀❀❀❀❀

For people who are facing death, this is the time, with appropriate engagement and facilitation, when they begin to let go of life itself. In our professional fields, we talk a lot about helping people *close* their lives, walking them through "the five things to say before you die, (forgive me, I forgive you, thank you, I love you, goodbye) or doing the hard process work of mending relationships before intentionally saying farewell and letting go. But I am talking about something more here, something underneath all that, something far harder to describe or even access—the quality of entrusting oneself to the timelessness of things, to the cosmic mysteries, to the ages. Truly letting go. When my close friend Jud died a few years back, he talked with me a lot about letting go, and how hard it was, and paradoxically, how gentle it became after he went into hospice care. Jud was a pediatrician and my colleague in hosting what was called Schwartz Center Rounds at my hospital, where the medical team members reflect on their own experiences in difficult cases. I won't soon forget Jud offering to use one of the rounds to talk with the audience, made up primarily of other physicians and nurses, about his own experience of diagnosis and slow decline. Jud died of pancreatic cancer, thirteen months later. On the morning of his death, knowing it was close, I went in to see him. I softly spoke his name and he roused enough to make knowing eye contact. And then as his lids fell back, he whispered to me, "is it time to let go now? Is it time to say goodbye?" "It is," I said. "Okay. Goodbye. I love you" were the whispered words that came back to me. And he had a slight smile on his lips as I left, which helped me feel confident of his grounding, and thus, in turn, I was better able to let *him* go. Interesting how that works.

In their book *Transforming Spirituality: Integrating Theology and Psychology,* F. LeRon Schults and Steven J. Sandage propose that the essential context for reflective meaning-making is the intimate encounter. Therapists and chaplains often talked about the quality of *presence,* of getting emotionally attuned to the patient's situation and sense of self. I'm actually talking about something deeper and more mutual here, having more to do with the mutual recognition of vulnerability, "looking into the abyss together" so to speak, establishing trust and connection that ultimately needs no words. Getting to that level becomes the essential grounding for any transformative learning and integration. This is a challenging thing to teach in spiritual care, which by definition is different from therapy in that it specifically does not attempt to maintain objectivity, but enters in deeply to the human condition, knowing one's own human frailty and therefore being able to identify fully with the patient. Every time I went in the room, I was mindful of my gratitude that it was not yet my turn or time to be the patient, and mindful as well of how close it is, how things could turn for me in a moment's notice. Meaningful spiritual care is always about moving toward intimacy, based on mutual recognition and vulnerability.

And then it is so important to be intentional. Again, this is much more than being a good listener. While establishing "presence" is essential, it is only a means to a deeper end. We want to focus on what we discern and sense in the other and raise the consciousness of the other about the ramifications of their reality and about the possibilities and potential that are unfolding. That also means tending to that which holds us in hopefully a faithful and loving communion, however the patient conceives of that. And if the patient's conceptions are self-limiting or coming out of dysfunctional adaptation to the pain of life, then it means re-directing toward that which is life-giving. The task is to make the implicit explicit, to be clear and intentional.

And, counter-intuitively, I am not interested in quieting things down (remember, we are talking about the dynamics of transformation here). Instead, we want to ramp things up, if gently and compassionately. What this means is that rather than see illness or trauma or loss as an isolated event, we set it in context as a part of the larger whole, as flowing out of all dimensions of life and as affecting all dimensions of life going forward, as reflective of the interrelatedness of the self as a system. It becomes a time for growing spiritual intelligence. We want to help the other, be it a loved one, a friend, a colleague or a patient, to get a grounding sense of place and creatureliness. We want to engage both the anxiety that comes with change and the possibilities that are emerging for spiritual healing, for deepening understanding, for growing the soul.

I really like the concept of reframing, which is essentially taking the patient's meaning framework and tilting it on its axis, so that what you see comes from a different perspective, and then sharing that with the patient. This notion reflects the biblical concept of dying to an old way of being and embracing a new way—a new way of seeing, of understanding, a process of capturing new possibility and new potential. And again, we get there by getting underneath convention and tradition, underneath the surface teachings of the religious tradition to their subtler and more nuanced intents.

For instance, many people struggle with a sense of inadequacy or defectiveness arising out of that quality of shame that gets established early in life due to experiences of marginalization and diminishment. If that stuff gets unwittingly perpetuated by the interactions with their faith tradition, then their spiritual framework becomes dysfunctional. If the "shoulds and oughts" of religion dominate in their thinking, then they would do well to begin to look at the core messages of their tradition in a new light. We want to shine that light into their darkness. Shining that light makes possible the seeing of new possibility and of making meaning. I've had a thousand conversations with people who have been damaged by their family and religious teachings. And they have needed to throw them out like old wine-skins and symbolically make new ones, ones that wouldn't spoil the new wine now being explored. And that exploration, in its fullest and deepest expression of reframing, leads into the awareness of interconnectedness, of becoming one with all things, both in life and death.

And that leads me into reflecting just a couple tenets that come out of Eastern thought: if we can engage existential suffering effectively and do the appropriate reframing, persons facing physical or emotional crises create the possibility of new understanding and transcendence of their condition. It has to do with seeing existential suffering as an expression of attachment to pleasure and to the ego, alongside the fear of the impermanent. As we embrace our spiritual interconnectedness with all things, it is consistent that there be a sense of letting go of all things to which we are attached in our consciousness, even our loved ones, and it has always been interesting to me how many people, as they decline toward death, tend to withdraw into quiet isolation and lack of communication, as if embracing this time-less destiny of detachment. It is the attachment—and the fear of losing the attachment—that generates the vulnerability to loss. And of course, not to get too technical, but this has to do with the difference between perceptual reality (that is, the experience of the physical nervous system) and fun-damental reality (which has to do with the infinite possibilities associated with universal consciousness and the continuity of life). Simply put, I try to not only embrace and accept my own finitude and thereby moderate my fear, but I try as well to embrace that reality for my wife and my children and my friends as well. When my father died unexpectedly in his early 70's, now a whole generation ago, my siblings were discomforted by my lack of emotion, as I gave thanks for his life and worked with my mind to accept his dying as natural and not-to-be-unexpected. I was certainly saddened, but the sense of devastation and abandonment and loss was muted by my inner knowing that such is the way of all things and that all things are in the care of the divine spirit.

It is that movement toward enlightenment (again, that is a purposeful word that is universal in all religions—the coming of light into the previous darkness of limited consciousness and attachment) that defines the process of reflection and exploration, with an increased sense of connection to the divine mysteries and the timelessness of existence being the outcome. In more traditional Western perspectives, we prefer to talk about the concepts of revelation and redemption. When Jesus taught about a "way" to greater connection to "the Father", it is the conclusion of most scholars that he was talking about essentially the same things as the eastern mystics—realizing a new spiritual pathway that would lead to greater god-consciousness and letting go of the things to which we are so attached, so that our "light" could be revealed more fully to the world. "Don't keep your light under a bushel," the story goes, for when it is allowed to shine, it will benefit those people who live in spiritual darkness. As things are "revealed" to us, as light is shined into our dim places, we assent to it and incorporate it into our faith frameworks; as we recognize our limitations and move into our humility and vulnerability, it is accompanied by feelings of hopefulness and renewal, and we see it as redemptive, that is, as meaningful and as the process for bringing something good out of something difficult.

In contemporary times, becoming somehow more enlightened has tended to orient us toward that which brings balance and congruence. Living a spiritually vital life today—and it doesn't really matter what language you use, being *faithful,* being *born again,* being *obedient and devout,* or just being *attuned to and appreciative of the mysteries*—is about having our inner reality reflected in our outer expressions, becoming more congruent, values-based, compassionate, understanding . . . , more *integrated,* if you will. So, rather than frame redemption as some non-understandable conception of something that happens to us, it becomes reflective of the possibilities that emerge out of the pain of life. When we become ill, or suffer trauma, our life first of all constricts. But when we work with it, we begin to see the new possibilities that emerge from the new spiritual path that seems to roll forward before us. Redemption is the hope that out of the pain of life, newness will emerge, a process that we traditionally describe as being divinely led.

The key to the process of renewal is to start by moving into confession, that is, first softening the heart, and then becoming honest about the choices made and the actions taken, seeking the settling down of the mind that comes only with real honesty and authentic self-disclosure. Not only does the soul seek health, it also seeks *confession* as a key pathway to health. Spiritual renewal and meaning-making are not about forgiveness as such, which the soul does not seek externally. Rather, it seeks to come clean, to confess. Think about it: when someone else pronounces a word of forgiveness about some hurt we may have caused, consciously or unconsciously, such a word only brings light into our shadows if it is internalized, if we forgive *ourselves.* When we compartmentalize our actions and thoughts and when we choose the easy path of self-deception, our soul continues to struggle. We tend to blow off words of forgiveness, or we may be grateful for them but fail to make any changes as a result. But without confession, we can't *breathe,* and where there is no breath there is no life.

That phrase became the powerful identifying phrase of the Black Lives Matter movement this last year, pointedly referring to the deaths of George Floyd and Eric Garner as their air was cut off while being subdued by the police. Indeed, it became the rallying cry of all such murders of Black men and women at the hands of unconscious white privilege and conscious white hate. Where there is no breath, there is no life, no future, no freedom, no ability to make meaning. The Black Lives Matter movement has awakened us, and attuned us to the abuses inherent in our culture and politics. Still today, half our leaders deny their own souls and support the big lie in an effort to retain power, cutting off the air of an entire nation.

The concept of forgiveness *follows* on confession, and only becomes meaningful when we have come clean. My favorite translation of the Greek word for forgiveness, "metanoia," is to *turn around*, to literally do an about face, to go back into the dynamics and actions that led to the hurtful behavior or alienation, and to work it through to reconciliation. Confession is the kick-starter. Reflection and learning are essential components. Humility and authenticity are key criteria to the movement and flow of healing. And forgiveness results, finally, when there is a change of heart, first in the offender, and then in the offended.

In sum, the key concepts in the dynamics of transformation apply to us all, and especially for people struggling with severe illness or who are caught in the existential suffering that is so much a part of the human condition. They are these:

- Engagement. This is not a passive process, we who care for them need to step in.

- Not empathy, but recognition and validation. We speak with people from alongside of them, as ones who intuitively know, who *get it*.

- Not disengaged support, but compassionate identification. Not only do we get it, but we recognize it as our own destiny, and we respond with compassion, even to resistance, even to difficult *acting out* behaviors.

- Reflection on experience to begin to make meaning and adapt to the new reality.

- Guiding the other toward a new pathway, seeing new possibilities and potential.

- Empowering them to act, to make the changes necessary to live into their new reality with courage and hope. This is a process "from below," that starts in the feelings, in the perceptions, in the not-yet-quite-conscious stuff that usually is based in some experience of hurt or fear. When it is brought forward and consciousness is raised, people generally want to change things, and begin to feel empowered, and begin to develop a new future story, moving, painfully, haltingly, and courageously, from darkness to light.

Again from Joan Chittister: "*The spiritual task of life is to feed hope. Hope is not something to be found outside of us. It lies in the spiritual life we cultivate within. The whole purpose of wrestling with life is to be transformed into the self we are meant to become, to step out of the confines of our false securities and allow our creating God to go on creating. In us.*[5]"

5. Chittister, *The Spirituality of Hope.*

Chapter Seven

Contemporary Theologies

"The soul given to each of us is moved by the same living spirit that moves the universe."

—ALBERT EINSTEIN, *EINSTEIN AND THE POET*

HOW DO WE, THEN, conceptualize and imagine the divine spirit? How do we talk about it rationally and constructively when it remains only something we sense, and then only in ways that remain mostly indescribable? We have been struggling to understand and make sense of our spirituality, and of our place in the universe ever since we developed the capacity to wonder and perceive and reflect. Throughout human history, we have imagined and speculated and studied what the heavens contain, we have developed stories and myths to make some semblance of order about it, and we have attached spiritual significance and images and powers to that which we imagined created it all. It is a maxim that we define ourselves in part by our attempts to define that which is beyond us, that from which we have been born, that which is wholly "other" than us. It is a process that has been in place since the very beginning. In the western world, as we have discussed, that took on the form of the theistic sky God, the one who created our world and directs our destinies from beyond us or from "above" us. Our conceptualizations of that creative, divine force evolved over four millennia, from Abraham's jealous and all-powerful Yahweh, to the God of love of the New Testament, embodied in the man-god Jesus. And in the course of that evolution, we defined ourselves as ones less than

God, as subservient, indeed as sinful and in need of God's redemption to set us right. Great religions grew up around these powerful frameworks for making meaning and for finding identity and our sense of belonging in the world, and each expression developed its own *theology*, its own explanation for understanding the divine energy that seems to create and sustain and empower and point the way for meaningful life.

But even as human consciousness began to discern that divine energy at work in the world and in the human heart and found it to be life-giving, human history also reflects how such conceptualizations morphed into expressions of oppression and control. As *theism* became viewed as the preferred understanding of how the world was created and how human life is supported or guided or directed, so did it become dogmatized. As key beliefs were articulated and then spread to become commonly held, they became culturally dominant, shaping like-minded communities and becoming self-sustaining. And as humans slowly organized themselves into villages and towns in order to farm and bake bread and brew beer, so did spiritual practices slowly get organized into community religions, either poly-theistic or mono-theistic. It is one of the mysteries of human life that we seem to struggle with that which is "known" but yet beyond our understanding, and instead we gravitate toward concreteness. When what we are trying to make communicable is beyond our ability to conceptualize, we seem to be at risk of ordering things in ways that run contrary to our experience, and that constrict rather than set free.

In the west, as the great religions of Christianity and Judaism and Islam evolved and took shape, they were accompanied by patriarchy and hierarchy within and perceived as threats to one another without. And while—at their best—they served and supported and created a spiritual grounding point for those within a tradition, so did they generate suspicion in each other. The vitriolic language and violent discrimination of Christian to Jew and Protestant to Catholic (and vice-versa) during the Middle Ages, together with the Reformation/Counter Reformation, laid the foundations for the schisms and distrust experienced within and between religions and even nations still today. Only recently has serious dialogue among differing religious groups begun to lead to deepened understanding, trust and cooperation.

Theism, at its inception, replaced the long-in-place, nature-based, understanding of the divine. As humans grew and expanded over the earth, and as competing groups were formed, and as we moved from being hunter/gatherers to becoming farmers and herders, and then as governments were formed and we began to compete for space and resources, it changed things. No longer was the earth perceived as the source of life and as a nurturing "mother;" now nature was seen as a gift from the sky God(s) given for our sustenance, as something for us to draw from, manage, and dominate. In turn, this shift gave rise to the concept of the "supremacy of man" to all things below, of humankind having dominion over the world while being subject to a divine being who is apart from nature. God was no longer seen as "in" nature, as in the pre-Christian goddess or tribal religions, but as "above" nature, and nature itself was de-divinized. Thomas Aquinas taught 750 years ago that the "wise ruler" ordinarily governs by delegation to competent subordinates, reflecting his theology, just as he perceived that the creator-God delegated to the inhabitants of creation. In Aquinas's articulation of Theism and Nature, God's ordinary providence governs by means of the regularities ("laws") built into nature. Unfortunately, the *natural laws* he defined tended to be perceived hierarchically. To be faithful was to honor the natural law and the creator-God above who set it all in motion. That perception remained central to orthodox theologies for the next twelve hundred years. But today, interestingly, it appears we may be coming full circle, back to where we started, with a growing conceptualization in the postmodern theologies, both inside and outside the church, that God is not only *in* the natural order, but that God indeed *is* the natural order, its energy, its life force, its very soul.

We are currently in the midst of a major paradigm shift, theologically, spiritually, culturally and socially. We are witnessing the deconstruction of traditional pre-enlightenment religious thought, and we may even be experiencing the front end of the disestablishment of the church and other traditional religious expressions, as we have come to know them. This is a postmodern reality, meaning that we are coming to comprehend the limits of human progress, the evolutionary dynamics at work in the cosmos, and the rapidly growing threat to our environment and to our very existence. We are moving from our premodern expressions of religion that were founded on the belief that God could be captured through sacred texts, rituals and spiritual experiences, through the modern understanding of critical methodologies and psychological theories, to the postmodern recognition that all knowledge about God and truth to this point has been provisional and socially constructed. We have learned that religious meaning more often arises out of heterogeneous social and moral contextual narratives than out of commonly held religious beliefs and practices. And we are learning that scientific exploration and imagination, rather than religious belief, may in fact be the primary pathway to enlightenment and understanding. Finally, the gap between faith and science may finally be closing.

Such a shift is both troubling and hopeful. It is troubling because of the slowly growing sense that the traditionally dominant triumphalist and deliverance theologies, born originally out of enslavement experiences and social oppression, were long ago co-opted and distorted by institutions of power. It is troubling because we are seeing that the reformers' attempts to deepen personal and communal spirituality while heightening a sense of freedom and intimacy with God were also grounded in myths arising from our inability to see beyond our immediate circumstances. It is troubling because of our growing sense that even our contextual theologies, emphasizing the divine spirit's transcendence and the transformation of the human heart that deepens the common good, such as the liberation theologies "from below" that emerged out of the struggle for justice in Central America, are inadequate to speak to our current circumstances and the threat of annihilation. Ultimately, it is troubling because it prompts a certain reorientation that is threatening to our traditional frameworks for making meaning. To deconstruct the beliefs that have shaped our history in such a way is painful, and it is likely a major contributing factor to the social split we are experiencing in America today, with those who hold to the tradition aligning with the political right, including some fundamentalists and white supremacists arming themselves with guns and promoting conspiracy theories.

Yet such movement and reorientation is so hopeful at the same time. When Galileo peered into his newly developed telescope and began to discern our real place in the universe and that it was *in motion*, and when Einstein recognized the creatively dynamic relationship of light and energy and mass, and when Watson, Crick and Franklin recognized the structure of the gene and the potential to unlock the genetic code and all that might mean, everything changed. The emphasis was no longer on what God had done, but on what God is at work *doing*. Now theologians and scientists both became engaged in exploring potential and possibility, and began to discern an unfolding and open future. Determinism gave way to freedom of choice which, in turn, gave rise to the recognition that all things are constantly changing and evolving and, thus, that we may even play a role in creating reality itself.

The theologian Sallie McFague has written that "the picture of reality coming to us from contemporary science is so attractive to theology that we would be fools not to use it."[1] It was the great philosopher Alfred North Whitehead who was among the first to embrace this new "picture of reality" and who framed it as a continuous expression of the divine spirit. He called it *process theology*,[2] because he perceived that creation was ongoing and that everything remained "in process." For Whitehead, process thought is based on the scientific conclusion that all reality is made up of "energy." Everything—God, ourselves, our world, our souls, our "spirits"—is energy at its quantum level, with sub-atomic particles constantly moving, constantly creating and being re-created, ever-flowing and ever-changing. The scientific discovery that matter is energy and that energy is matter changed completely how we understood the processes of creation and evolution. And the discovery that reality actually changes when electrons collide *and* a new electron is created in addition (Whitehead's famous maxim that *the many become one and are increased by one*) led to the recognition that every moment contains the potential for new possibilities to emerge as a result. And the more recent discovery that any such electrons *remain in relationship* (what Templeton Prize winner George Ellis has termed *kenosis*[3]) even after being split out of an atom, and then even across unlimited time and space, suggests that the possibilities are oriented toward maintaining relationship come what may, and toward building up life rather than breaking it down. Whitehead called this *the attraction of ideals*, and extrapolated that all of reality is in God's sphere of influence and that the future is open, filled with redemptive potential, ours for the co-creating.

In process theology, the world is made up of energy "events," where the dynamic flow of energy creates all that is, and all that *is* is constantly being re-created. And the "aim" or impulse or purpose behind the energy flow comes from the Source of Life that we refer to as "God," and which brings together energy events *in response to our needs and desires*, providing an "inrush" of data and feeling that creates influence and shapes the unfolding of the future. This was both a timeless and a radical reinterpretation of long-standing beliefs—that the divine spirit creates new things in *response* to our desires. This is a *relational* theology, where individual events arise out of the divine spirit being in relationship with us, a relationship that

1. McFague, Quoted in O'Murchu, *Quantum Theology*, 3.
2. Whitehead, *Process and Reality*.
3. Ellis, *Intimations of Transcendence*.

does not end merely by us splitting ourselves away from that spirit, just as electrons from the same atom maintain relationship despite their at times violent separations. This is a theology where the spirit is *for* us, in relationship with us at all times, unconditionally, as the source of the "aim" of the energy and as the one who knows all potentialities. Whitehead would say that God chooses the best possible potential for us and offers it (as feeling, intuition, discernment) as the initial aim. This is God as transcendent creator—that which calls creative moments into being and invites us into relationship, into participation in the process. We respond or not. We are free to co-create or to turn away. But with every unfolding moment, God offers the next aim, "feeling" the outcome of every occasion, constantly seeking our fullest potential, always aiming for maximum intensity of feeling and the grandest expression of beauty possible. It is as if the divine spirit is never reactive and always responsive, as if when we say no, or turn away from what is offered, yet another offer is provided, as if God is saying, "Okay then, how about *this*?" in a never-ending flow of love and grace.

Process thought is a theology where God's power is regarded as persuasive rather than coercive. As opposed to the "theist" image of the lawmaker sky-god, or the "deist" image of the clockmaker who sets us on a mechanistic, predetermined path, this is an image of God where God's power lies in the dynamic *attraction of ideals* within relationship, where God is always calling us into connection, always creating new possibilities. In fact, Whitehead would say that this is the fullest expression of love: that God remains "intimately" involved with us in all feelings and events, integrating all experiences, forever giving rise to new aims, wanting us to become the best that we can become. God is seen as a life force of genuine love, as a movement of energy that flows forward and points the direction toward fullness of life, even stimulating in us the desire that we know well-being and harmony and fulfillment.

It is consistent then, in process theology, to claim that God is not off in the distant sky, "apart" from us somehow, but that the divine spirit is imbued in all things: nature, the world, the cosmos, us; that we, in fact, are "in" God as God is in us and in all things. As it is written in the book of the Acts of the Apostles in the Christian scriptures: God . . . "is not far from each one of us. For 'in God we live and move and have our being . . . for we too are God's offspring.'"[4]

4. NRSV, *Acts* 17:27–28.

This redefines our spiritual natures and practices and ways of being. If the divine spirit is indeed a life source that pervades and is inherently present in all things, constantly creating and renewing and transforming our reality, then we need to rethink some things. As an example, it would have significant ramifications for how we pray. If, from a non-theistic perspective, God is not a person or being who functions in an anthropomorphic way, who is understood not as a being that will listen and respond to my prayers, then what is the purpose of prayer? Who would I be praying to? In fact, if God is not a person, then how can persons be expected to have *any* kind of relationship with a non-personal deity? The answer for those of us who are non-theists requires a discussion of what prayer is to begin with—a discussion, I dare say, religious organizations need to have. If prayer is a transaction, like a long-distance call or a form of communication between humans and a divine spirit that "hears" them and chooses how to respond—and then only does so seemingly based primarily on the goodness or faithfulness of the one praying, or on the "seriousness" of need—then prayer doesn't make a whole lot of sense, even though that is the dominant way of thinking about it in American religion. Most of us know intuitively that prayer doesn't have a cause and effect quality, since we have had to come to grips with the reality that loss and death and tragedy and natural disasters have their way with all of us, no matter what. There is no "deliverance" from the pain of life and from our own human finitude.

In process thought, however, rather than prayer being seen as a transaction, we might look at it as a spiritual expression that helps us connect to the divine mysteries, that opens us up to acceptance and that shores up our courage, and when we pray like that, it becomes a powerful and meaningful act. If prayer is a self-conscious act of humility, to empty oneself in silent meditation by holding open empty space, or by offering trembling and carefully chosen words that allow us, and perhaps others, to overhear ourselves seeking higher ground, then prayer can become to our minds what poetry is to the soul. We move into the authentic human expressions of honesty, vulnerability, hope, and a deeper and more profound trust.

Non-theist prayer is vulnerable speech, not transactional speech; it doesn't look for anything, it doesn't expect a response. And yet it changes things. It changes our emotions, our attitudes, our awareness. It may even—through the expression of our desires—influence the unfolding of our reality in ways we can't fully comprehend but that reflect the processes of creation and life at the quantum level (see below). When we pray as a spiritually meditative expression of our authentic human needs and desires and hopes and dreams, our hearts open to the possibility of transformative love and a new future, and things begin to coalesce. And the divine that is *in* us—not separate from us—speaks *through* us and *to* us, creating possibility and the potential for something new.

❀ ❀ ❀ ❀ ❀

Process theology was a radical departure from Neo-orthodoxy, which had attempted to integrate *into* the tradition new insights gained from the historical-critical approach to scriptural studies. The tradition itself was being transformed, the quest for the historical Jesus was well underway, and the true meaning of his death and resurrection for contemporary faith was being fully engaged. That has led to the growing recognition in the postmodern era that the theism that defines the Christian tradition is in decline. The question facing the church—and the culture that was founded, in part, on expectations of conformity to theistic creeds and constructs—is whether or not it can let go of what author and theologian Marvin E. Bryce has called "the coping mechanism of theistic religion."[5] In its place, we are being invited to embrace the growing self-consciousness that would enable us to relate openly and deeply to that in which our being is grounded, and that which is part of who we are and yet somehow more than who we are. To do so would be to look to the teachings of Jesus and to frame the Christ-story as a calling to a higher order of being and as a personal engagement that empowers what Tillich called "the courage to *be*."

Could it be that Jesus revealed the divine through his call to follow the "way" of love and reverence for all and how he embodied that way of being in his own life, knowing fully well where it would lead for him? Could it be that the theological meaning of the crucifixion is that it exposed our response to that call to a self-sacrificing and *giving* life, that is, that it revealed our *resistance* to life in God? Could it be that we—all of us who get caught in wanting to protect our world views and the statues quo—just couldn't find the courage to take in the vision he espoused or the maturity to which he called us? Could it be that we were so threatened by his truth-telling and by his radical teachings about the path to integration and fulfillment and meaning, that we had to just eradicate him? When Pontius Pilate is described as "washing his hands" of him, it symbolically captured the angst of being unable to tolerate his voice and his vision.

5. Bryce, *Challenge to the Church*, 126.

Former Episcopalian Bishop John Shelby Spong has been perhaps the most prominent of the many authors and researchers and theologians who have written and spoken about these perspectives over the last two decades, now becoming the dominant construct of progressive Christianity and a key component of increased spiritual intelligence. In his books *Why Christianity Must Change or Die* and *Biblical Literalism: A Gentile Heresy*, among others, he notes that far from the old distorted theistic story of God somehow sacrificing his own son to atone for our sins, the story of Jesus is really a beautiful story of love transforming abusive power and of setting aside selfish needs to serve others as the way to fullness with God. As our consciousness has evolved, and as our knowledge has increased, we have come to see that the real story is about the call to live into the realm of God—a call which for Jesus was spoken in life and fully revealed through his death—that generates a profound sense of "recognition" of God's intent for all humanity. This then becomes the true Easter story: breaking the bonds of spiritual death to live fully in God and to have God live fully in us, *in life*—and in that which is before and beyond life. The work that Jesus was truly about was enhancing life for all he encountered; it was about enhancing love and truth and justice for all; it was about calling us to a higher consciousness rooted in the divine spirit.

This changes everything. The modern era and the theistic tradition led to the inevitability of meaninglessness. The concepts handed down from previous generations have simply not been adequate to stem the proliferation of alienation and spiritual confusion that has arisen in the face of growing complexity and threat. And perhaps alienation from self has been the greatest cost, exposed by growing psychological and spiritual illnesses. Today in the United States, one in four adults have used anti-depressant medication in an effort to alter their brain chemistry, skewed by repeated insults to self-esteem. Suicide is epidemic. Eating disorders in our adolescents have emerged as a new expression of the struggle for meaning, as the addictive dynamics of older generations have been driven down to our young. Opiate addiction remains rampant, driven in part by out-for-profit pharmaceutical companies. Elected governmental leaders in Congress go against their own moral code in attempts to maintain the illusion of power. And the communities that have traditionally given us the grounding and the support to cope with and adapt to change are rapidly changing themselves, with troubling trends of fostering exclusivity rather than generativity and self-giving love, and of promoting a message far different than the gospel of

Jesus that for centuries gave rise to communities of care and inclusion and tolerance. Note the dysfunction and corruption of evangelical Christianity. Finding the "way" to fullness in God may be a more crucial question than ever before.

❖ ❖ ❖ ❖ ❖

As the scientific field of physics began to explore and theorize about quantum mechanics under Albert Einstein, the conclusions being reached also stimulated re-thinking about God, divine energy and reality. Quantum mechanics attempts to explore and understand the "organic fields of energy" at every level of the universe. As discoveries were made about the nature of light and energy, as the sub-atomic world began to open up through application of theory to discoverable data, and as the universe began to be understood as dynamic, expanding and ever-evolving, theology changed again. The traditional construct of theism began to just seem out of touch.

Building on process theology, quantum theology emerged in the early 2000s as an expression of what has come to be called "the new universe story." That story grows out of continuing discovery about creation itself, about the Big Bang and the birth of the cosmos, about the laws of gravity and the speed of light and the theories of relativity, giving rise to speculation about the existence of the invisible dark matter and dark energy that shape the ongoing evolution of all things. Extrapolating from quantum mechanics, theologians began to conclude that built into the story is a certain *intentionality* toward life. Things had to work "just so" in order for life to emerge. And the quickly-dawning realization that such processes are at work throughout the universe—a universe far larger than ever imagined in earlier centuries—changed the paradigm radically. Now God was no longer solely concerned with us but with *all* things, no longer a sky God but now a universe God, no longer a *personal* God per se, but now a transcendent *and* imminent experience of loving energy, dynamically present at every level of existence, moving intentionally, offering an experience of transformation that *becomes* profoundly personal *as it is experienced*. In this new vision God creates all things, is in all things and imbues all things with energy; God is known in the heavens and known as well in the quanta particles that serve as the building blocks of all that is. And we are only beginning to comprehend, through our evolving consciousness, what this means.

Imagine that moment, some three billion years ago or so, when a simple primitive cell mutated and began to capture light from the sun in the process of photosynthesis. Envision, for a moment, how the molecules of chlorophyll absorbed photons from the sun, which enabled them to convert that energy into food (sugar) for themselves, and how they then drew in molecules of water and carbon dioxide while emitting new oxygen molecules. We now know that the toxic atmosphere of the early earth became transformed with a rapid "spewing forth" of oxygen, and the possibilities for life blossomed exponentially. And we can begin to comprehend how the earth began to "receive" the sunlight so freely given, utilizing it in a new way, resulting in this radically new thing called life. We have since learned that the sun converts four million tons of its mass into energy in the form of light *every second*, never to be recaptured, given as energy to feed the universe, and as a result, we live. And there are trillions of suns and billions of galaxies.

Karl Rahner, the great Catholic theologian, has called this radiating light "one continuous act of grace," and "God's self-communication"—an outpouring of the very being of God that not only permeates but maintains all life.[6] In this story, the Incarnation (the story of Jesus) is understood by Rahner as the breaking through of God's Light into human consciousness. Through Jesus and his deep discernment of the realm of God, we became enlightened in a way never before experienced. It was an evolutionary leap, prompted by God's gracious intentionality. In a parallel process to photons and chlorophyll birthing Life itself, Jesus was able to "absorb" the radiance of God in a way that transformed Jesus himself and all who were in his presence, birthing a new level of consciousness about the divine intent and providing a new framework for living meaningfully.

The theories of quantum mechanics are helping us to begin to recognize that we are all connected, all a part of a cosmogenesis that continues to unfold over eons, that acknowledges evolution as a creative process urged on from within and without by the very Spirit of God. It recognizes that through the human species, the consciousness of the cosmos is itself evolving, and that all is intended to enhance life and love. It may be, in fact, that it is our growing consciousness that is the essential component of co-creating the future with God, of bringing into being a new reality or of discerning what many in the field understand to be alternative realities. Such is the divine mystery unfolding before us, a mystery that invites us into a new and deeper spirituality that holds the promise of fullness of life in and through the divine spirit.

6. Rahner, quoted by Leijssen in Louvain Studies, *"Grace as God's Self-Communication."*

✺✺✺✺✺

Smaller than the small, I am that still center within you,
That needle's eye through which all the threads of the universe are
drawn.
Perhaps you think you know me, but you do not know me.
Of everything that is, of every word that is spoken on the lips or in
the heart,
Of every thought and hope and wish, I am the silent witness.
Nearer to you than ecstasy in the blood yet more mysterious far,
I am the guardian of every color that catches the eye,
Of every taste that pleases the tongue, of every word that speaks to
the heart.
Perhaps you think you know me, but you do not know me.
Mine is the voice that sings out of the voiceless night,
That rises like music out of the root of the dark thorn,
Out of the lucid throat of the fountain.
Smaller than small, I am the seed of all that is known and
unknown.
I am the root and stem of meaning, the ground of wonder.
Through me, each tendril of desire is drawn and breathes in con-
sciousness of Being.
And yet when you open your ears to my voice and
Listen with all your hearing, and listen again,
No subtle joining of notes and words,
No vertical song is heard.
But silence is singing.
And when you open your eyes to my appearance but cannot see me
Or when you close your eyes, or close your ears
In concentration and look with your hands
And turn back again the pages of sleep's dark scripture,
No great or terrible sign awakes, no vision burns.
But absence is shining.
Mine is the secret that lies hidden like the lustrous pearl
Gleaming within its oyster.
The deepest secret,
The secret hidden within the secret.
—Unknown

Chapter Eight

The Quest

"Do not be daunted by the enormity of the world's grief. Do justly, now. Love mercy, now. Walk humbly, now. You are not obligated to complete the work, but neither are you free to abandon it."

—*THE TALMUD*

I LEARNED THE ART of spiritual care through many and varied painful experiences, and over a long time. I learned it from my patients, from my reading, from my peers, from talking about and reflecting on my experiences with astute colleagues and teachers, from always trying to deepen my understanding and appreciation of what others were going through. And, I learned it, in part, from my friend Jud, whom I wrote about earlier. I got to know Jud (the one who died from pancreatic cancer) first as a golfing partner, one of a foursome of neighbors that would play a few times every summer in my early 50s. He was always keenly interested in my work as a hospital chaplain and hungry to discuss human issues in his role as a physician as he was transitioning from pediatric medicine to the newly emerging medical specialty of palliative care. Walking from green to tee and sipping a beer at the 19th hole was most often accompanied by discussion of a current case in the hospital, his or mine, as he found himself more and more wanting to work with adults who were facing chronically painful illnesses and death. As things happen, we both ended up working at the same medical center, where we became close friends and colleagues, notable for our regular drop-in chats in his or my office. It was Jud's idea to initiate Schwartz Center Care Rounds in our hospital. Schwartz Center Rounds, as noted above, focus on the experience and reflections of the care providers, and are wonderful teaching opportunities. We flew out to Boston together to get facilitator training, where we talked at length and in depth about our evolving viewpoints and our desire to work on a deeper level with our patients, and about our own mortality and ways of making meaning.

Our first rounds at the hospital featured a young female oncologist, reflecting on her care of a 42 year old mother of three, from initial diagnosis of metastatic breast cancer, to her death a short eight months later. It had been a rocky and painful journey for both physician and patient, neither of whom described themselves as "spiritual or as espousing any particular faith perspective." Unique to the case discussion was the physician's sense that as the patient more and more resisted the inevitability of her death, demanding that the people around her always be positive and resolved to get her better, the physician herself became more and more conflicted and personally reflective, wondering how best to care for her patient. The oncologist then related that on the day when death finally came, the patient had demanded yet one more round of now-ineffective chemotherapy, and that she, the physician, had provided it, even while knowing it would bring no benefit. Then, through tears and with heartfelt regret, she talked about "not telling her patient the truth" about the progression of the cancer, and about her "failure" to care for her effectively. It was a profoundly powerful moment in the rounds, and all of us listeners felt deeply privileged to be let into such intimate reflections. After a moment of quiet, as we all tried to come to grips with what we had just heard, I turned to the audience and asked a standard Schwartz Center question, "Has anyone here had a similar experience?" We had about a hundred people gathered in the auditorium. A hand slowly went up in the back, and I brought the mic to him—the chief of oncology, our presenter's boss. He started by saying, "I want to tell you about the first time I lied to a patient . . . ," but then he began to choke up and had to stop to gather himself before going on. And it felt like we were all standing on holy ground. And I looked at Jud, with tears in his eyes, and he nodded and smiled, as if to say, "this is what we trained for, this is what we want, this is the sacred stuff of medicine."

The next month, three staff members of our eating disorders unit presented for the rounds. The case focused on one of the physicians who worked with eating disordered patients, who was both angry and tearful about her inability to break through to a twenty-three year old gay man who had ended up dying from extreme malnutrition. He had been through the treatment program twice, totally resistant to doing the necessary internal work to work through his illness, an illness that was indicative of his profound psychic woundedness and isolation. We could have talked for hours about him. But Schwartz Center Rounds focuses on the medical care providers, and so we engaged with the physician. She talked about her powerlessness, about the futility of not being able to make a difference with that patient, about her own psychic pain of growing up with high expectations and her own awareness of her driven-ness and perfectionism. One of the nurses took the mic and gently said, "I always had the sense that the two of you (the physician and the twenty-three-year-old man) were not all that different from each other." It was not something that ever would have been said outside of those rounds. And we all waited with bated breath. The doc was silent for a long time. You could see her wrestle with and slowly work through her emotions. Then she nodded her head and said in a very soft voice, "I guess it's time for me to let go of some things . . . ."

We went on to talk about how hard it is for "healers" to embrace the reality that some patients die, and the social worker then spoke about her journey of learning to stay compassionate toward those patients that were seemingly self-destructive. When I asked the doc to reflect a bit on how she found meaning in her work, she acknowledged that putting all her eggs in the basket of "recovery" wasn't working very well, and she wasn't sure about where to look going forward. But I sensed a new beginning when, after the rounds ended, I saw her walk over to the nurse who had gently confronted her, put her arms around her, and thank her sincerely for her honesty.

Holy ground. Deep intimacy. Compassionate acceptance. Openness. Truth-telling. Meaning-making. The privilege of honest connection, of trust, of hope, of gratitude. Jud and the countless others who went before deepened my life and attuned me to how I wanted to be in the world, and what I wanted to do. I was growing *down*. That is, I was slowly coming into the awareness of the importance of facing the deep and painful realities of life and the human condition straight on, perhaps a bit tentatively, but with a new sense of purpose, working to find the courage to stand on the edge of the abyss and embrace both the emptiness and the opportunity. I was slowly realizing that the pathway forward for me as a clinician and educator was "down and in," into my own brokenness and shadows, into my deep and still too-hidden sense of self, into the messy and difficult "unintegrated" places of my true being.

I remember the first time I looked closely into the viscera of a surgical patient in the OR. She had been laid open from sternum to pubis as the surgeon sought out the cancer that had invaded her, cutting and pushing and invading. And I knew I had to undergo a metaphorically similar process to get inside myself, to explore unresolved and disparate feelings, to go down and in, in order to open up and experience healing and move toward greater wholeness. I came, in fact, to honor and accept the process of *debridement*, which is a surgical term for the process of cutting away necrotic tissue in patients with skin ulcers and wounds that won't heal on their own. Debridement allows for healing to happen from below, as the body gradually recreates itself under the damaged area. And many patients would need to have their deep physical wounds debrided repeatedly, enduring significant repetitive pain. If I was to become an effective spiritual care provider, I would need to undergo the debridement of my emotional wounds. It is paradoxical to say that a key component of waking up to higher consciousness and awareness—of truly making meaning—can only come through the journey of self-reflection that leads to greater personal and professional integration. Such was the journey of growing down to deepened awareness and acceptance and understanding.

Such self-reflection is, however, only a part of the necessary process of awakening required to become truly rooted in what gives our lives meaning. The other key component is becoming attuned to that which "speaks" to us from outside the self. This is how we define spirituality: the intentional attunement to that which is beyond us and within us and around us which brings life and perspective and meaning. After having been a professional parish pastor for eight years, I was now finally beginning to learn what was necessary for a meaningful spiritual life: intentionality—to look for and search for that which brings insight and awareness and perspective; to begin to trust that that which is *more* than us is what gives meaning to our lives. In his spiritually revolutionary writings, the wonderful author Eckhart Tolle points us toward that *"higher level of consciousness"* and that *"vast realm of intelligence beyond thought"* that brings into us the joy and beauty and love and meaning of life.[1] He suggests we seek to get out of our own thoughts into our "observer mind" and awaken to that which is beyond us and so much more than us.

1. Tolle, "You Are Not Your Mind," 14.

Writers and prophets and mystics and leading thinkers have written about spiritual intentionality and spiritual care for eons. So, our own spirituality and the provision of spiritual care can both be thought about here as the reflective expressions of persons looking together at the painful realities of life and intentionally trying to come to grips with them and set them in the universal context of life, and it has been practiced as long as humankind has been mindful of the mysteries of living and dying. It is referenced over and over in the Psalms and written about throughout the Sufi (Islamic) and Hebrew and Christian scriptures. It is a subject of poetry and discourse and contemplation among writers and teachers and preachers throughout history, from the desert fathers to medieval nuns to professors and preachers and presidents. From Jesus to Lao Tzu, from Hildegard of Bingen to Herman Hesse, from Florence Nightingale to Paul Kalanithi (the wonderful physician-author of *When Breath Becomes Air*), from Lincoln to Biden, spiritual care is named as forming the foundation of coping with illness and finding consolation and hope amidst the difficulties and challenges of life. Martin Luther wrote extensively about it in the 1500s, as the work of "sustaining, healing, reconciling, and guiding" one another in the face of illness and loss. Martin Luther King Jr., his namesake, taught that spiritual care was the essential component of overcoming racism and oppression. A profoundly natural human expression, it is born out of our inclination to enter into caring relationships to assuage our own aloneness and the isolation we see in others. And it is as much a part of our history and genetic makeup as our desire to perceive and discern the workings of the divine and face the uncertainties of the future with hope.

I have always wanted to understand more fully, to see through the veil more clearly, to discern the movement of the divine and to obtain greater insight into human experience and the process for making meaning. I have always been aware of the desire to perceive what is really going on in nature, in creation, in the world and throughout the universe. I have been fascinated by the flow of energy, by what makes us tick, by the diversity of belief systems and life philosophies, by how we evolved our morals and ethics and our frameworks for living, by history and psychology and illness and medicine. And I have been drawn to explore illness and dying, and the existential realities of our mortality, since it is often only at that point that we address the most difficult dimensions of our lives. On that level, I gradually came to see that engaging in spiritual care is about staring into the depths with one another and then seeking to quiet the feelings that come up in the face of our finitude, seeking to "make sense" of things.

I came to understand that making sense of things is most often about being with and speaking with those now caught up in dealing with loss, suffering, illness, pain and encroaching death. But it is not only about that. Spiritual care in its fullest expression captures what has been a consistent struggle throughout human history to put into words *meaningful* responses to the human emotions that get generated in the face of powerful experiences, not just those that cause suffering and sorrow, but those that spark joy and gratitude as well. It is about how we try to make sense of our world, how we try to comfort and sustain and uplift and encourage one another, how we look to the unseen for guidance and understanding, how we creatively and sensitively try to engage the breadth and depth of the human experience. It was a natural fit for me, and would become a lifetime pursuit.

❀ ❀ ❀ ❀ ❀

Kurt was typical of our resident students when he entered our program—capable, bright, and responsible. He was a married 30 year old, a seminary graduate from a conservative protestant tradition, with the advantage of considerable training in marriage and family therapy. We had him work as a chaplain in behavioral health for six months and then moved him into the cardiac care program. By all surface accounts, he excelled. He was well-liked by the nurses, a leader in his cohort, and he functioned with a high level of autonomy. He was also a reflective thinker, and as trust deepened between us, he more openly shared his felt inadequacy, his anxiety, his encroaching agnosticism, and his dissatisfaction with his role. Kurt had moved past feeling inadequate to speak to the suffering he encountered; now he was frustrated by the silence of his peers and even of the other medical professionals with whom he worked in the clinical setting. A particularly painful case was unfolding for him, involving a declining, older woman, unable to guide her own care due to her encephalopathy, on full life support, including a ventilator and dialysis.

The patient's family—of a minority culture—had long since been alienated from the medical and nursing personnel who saw them as reactive and making poor choices. It was a classic case of ineffective communication, painful assumptions, and polarized distrust. And Kurt quickly came to the realization that his silence was contributing, along with everyone else's, to prolonging what had become an unacceptably horrific situation.

He "confessed" his struggle to me, and together we tried to discern how to bring light to this particular darkness.

The painful script of what we knew as "benign paternalism" (which was anything but) was played out again in a care conference the next day. After failing one more time to motivate the family to allow the withdrawal of life support, the physician threatened to walk out and to "sign off" the case, clearly frustrated. He had unwittingly put the family in the untenable postmodern position of having to "make a decision" to end their mother's life, while they felt distrustful, alienated and abandoned.

It was at that point that Kurt spoke to them all, directly and compassionately. He lifted up the narrative of the patient's life, acknowledged that no one should ever be asked to take responsibility for the moment of death of a loved one, asked the physician to recommend the course that was in the best interests of his patient, and stood with the family in their angst and isolation. He later related that as he spoke he had tears in his eyes and a quiver in his voice, reflecting the depth of his conviction that such "over and against-ness" would not be allowed to continue. And it became a moment that lent truth to the adage that *when the word (of truth, of compassion, of love) is spoken, the spirit is set free.* Within the hour, the family had Kurt paged, asking him to tell the physician they would prefer to have their mother "released from the bondage" she was experiencing. And "would he gather with them all for prayer?" He would, in full voice.

Such experiences are not atypical in our medical centers. Being admitted to a hospital with a serious progressive illness, or in old age with a debilitating condition, or as one is approaching the end of a long journey through a terminal illness, can be tantamount to entering a spiritual wasteland. And too often people are unwilling to talk meaningfully with each other, and families are locked into lifelong patterns of silence. Many such stories have stayed with me.

When Sarah came into the hospital by ambulance, she was in cardiogenic shock, following a large myocardial infarction. As the medical team sought to stabilize her over the next couple of days, they determined that Sarah would likely not survive long without being placed on a ventricular assist device as a bridge to a heart transplant. At that time, surgically implanting a VAD was a high risk procedure with relatively poor outcomes. During those first forty-eight hours, I sought to connect with her husband, Joe, and to her two kids, both in their twenties. Joe, who was understandably traumatized and anxious, wanted to proceed with the surgery as soon as possible. Sarah, who slowly became alert and able to communicate, was less sure, her eyes betraying her fear. On the third day, the docs asked me to talk with her.

Sarah received me immediately. She teared up and took my hand when I told her I was the chaplain. Joe had told me that her faith was extremely important to her and that she would want prayers, but I discovered quickly that Sarah was not just a faithful woman, she was also a gracious and loving woman of significant depth and awareness. Sarah wanted more than prayers; she wanted to understand her situation, and to well up her courage and her trust, and to ask me to tend to her family if she died. She understood fully well that she was hanging by a single thread. And Sarah took me in, powerfully, and I was mindful of the profound privilege. We had to communicate around the ventilator that enabled her to breathe, but she was intent on doing so, occasionally scrawling out words and phrases, sometimes mouthing words, always communicating her feelings through her eyes, nodding or shaking her head with purpose. Sarah became one of my teachers as I grew quickly in profound appreciation of her wisdom and thoughtfulness. And, of course, I became significantly attached. I wanted to do all I could for her to help her rest and ultimately, to help her survive.

And then she told me that she was afraid for Joe, that she knew he would need help, especially if she didn't survive, that he always leaned on her for emotional strength. True to form, she was more concerned about her family than herself, accepting the reality of her condition. And indeed, I had come to understand that Joe, who was a new car salesman and manager, sought to maintain a positive face at all times, stating his confidence that God would "see her through" and that everything would be all right. There was no room in Joe's psyche at the time to let in negative thoughts or doubt.

And then Sarah's daughter asked if she could speak to me in private. She expressed the same concerns about her father that her mother had, cueing me into Joe's struggle with alcohol, his "tender heartedness" but also his tendency to become rageful, noting a few incidents of physical abuse toward her brother, followed by effusive apologies over the years. She asked me to help him.

Joe was not about to become vulnerable with me, other than to ask me for prayers. It was as if he needed to maintain his own thin thread of false optimism and denial in order to continue on. Like so many others over the years, he used religious language to avoid true reflection and connection.

I ached for Joe, wanting him to talk realistically and intimately with his wife, wanting him to support her and express his love for her and face the realities together. But it was something he just couldn't manage. He would hold her hand and speak reassurances, but he didn't want Sarah to see his fear or his dependence on her. He gave her a thumbs up when she went into the operating room. But, as is too often the case, Sarah endured the surgery, only to remain alive for about twenty-four hours. She died surrounded only by strangers, never having regained consciousness. When Joe was told that his wife had expired, he immediately left the hospital, leaving his daughter and his son alone with the nurses to start to make the funeral arrangements.

Joe and Sarah's story was archetypal. Their struggle to come to grips with radical change and to care for each other under extreme circumstances, together with their inability to share it intimately and make meaning from it, was representative of hundreds of cases over the years. I came to deeply appreciate, on the one hand, the human quest to survive, and the struggle to make sense of things, and the effort required to find ways to carry on and endure, to maintain some sort of hope and reason to trust the unfolding. But I also came to appreciate the power of resistance and self-protection and the oft-times extreme reluctance to face reality. Such is the human condition. In light of both of those realities, I also learned that the tools of traditional chaplaincy were wanting. Facile words and memorized prayers were insufficient. Health care was changing. Religious expression was changing. And I was changing—learning, growing, struggling myself to make sense of things and better engage the painful realities that confronted me. We needed to find better ways to be with one another, I realized; we needed to forge a different way of framing such challenges, a pathway forward that could generate authentic hope and acceptance, not just lightweight optimism.

Perhaps the reason this story has stayed with me so powerfully is because of its amazing postscript. It was a year later, on the anniversary of Sarah's death as it turned out, that Joe came unexpectedly to my office in the hospital to find me. "Will you help me?" he asked. Absolutely. And his journey *down and in* began anew.

❄ ❄ ❄ ❄ ❄

Standing with physicians imparting grim prognoses to newly ill patients; holding 24-week fetuses in my hands as they expired; having my hands clutched by elderly COPD patients as they approached their last breaths;

being caught up in the juxtaposition of the sorrow of the family graciously if painfully donating the heart of their eighteen-year-old son now brain dead from a diving accident, only to move to the overwhelming joy of the recipient in the next unit only hours away from fatal heart failure—every experience affected me deeply. And then there were the many, many experiences of withdrawing ventilators, stopping dialysis, foregoing another round of chemotherapy, and taking out feeding tubes . . . ; such were the moments that changed my life. Experiences like those touch us deeply and shift our thinking and, for me, it's been a natural lead-in to trying to figure out what's in everyone's best interest and what's fair and what's reasonable, or how much suffering any one person should endure, or how to engage conflict in a collaborative and compassionate manner, trying to work through the power differentials, recognizing we are all on the same page in these struggles.

And what makes it challenging is that the cultural guidelines aren't very clear. What ought we use to shape the decisions we make when facing a declining or dying patient, or medically futile circumstances? One of my favorite writers, the medical sociologist Arthur Frank, reminds us it's not enough just to turn to the patient. Often, they (or their families) are the ones least able to provide the guidance. When we ask somebody if they want to continue with aggressive intervention—something we routinely do by the way, especially in the face of grave prognoses and intense suffering—we are likely to experience profound courage and immense strength, or at least an adamant refusal to stop. After all, its deeply imbedded in our national ethos and no one wants to let anyone down, neither their physician nor their families, and so the reactive response tends to be to fight on. I've seen remarkable resiliency and fortitude in such moments, though it's a rare thing at the end stages of a chronic, progressive illness for that to lead to any kind of a long-term positive outcome. But the harsh reality is that more often than not the suffering is merely prolonged, and everyone slowly wears down, including the care-providers, in no small part because we look not to our own discernment and wisdom and skill but to the patient or their family—now desperate or withdrawn or, more frighteningly, empty of spirit or will to live—to guide the treatment plan, dare I say too often sacrificing the full truth of their situation for well-intended but misplaced efforts at honoring autonomy.

And why do we do that? Perhaps it's because we all feed into the now-dominant narrative of illness in western culture, which Frank refers to as "the myth of restitution."[2] And it's a soul-less narrative. The myth of restitution goes like this: "I was well, now I am sick, but with modern medicine and your help I will be well again." Add to that script that classic American dynamic of entitlement, captured by the belief that "I have a right to whatever it takes to get me well," and you can see we have a recipe for very expensive and not terribly humane end-of-life and high-tech care. And there's one more part to the myth of restitution—the overlay of powerless victim and heroic rescuer—a dimension that has become especially problematic in the culture of medicine. If the reward that most tertiary care physicians are reporting in the statistical surveys is accurate, then physicians themselves would be the least likely to attach the descriptor "heroic" to their work. It's difficult work because it's become so impersonal.

In the restitution narrative, we have misplaced the term. To do one's job well and thoroughly is an excellent accomplishment and reflective of professionalism, but it is not heroic. But to bear the suffering that illness and its remedies can bring *can* be heroic. It is a term that, rightly understood, ought only be applied to the one bearing up under the disease, the patient and the patient's family. Such heroism (and again, we all know intuitively what it looks like) produces in each of us a deep sense of sorrow, if we're in touch and staying in tune with our souls. It is a deep, aching, compelling sorrow that breaks our hearts even while it motivates and empowers our resolve to understand and to love—and even to help people die good deaths, if there be such a thing.

So, the dominant illness narrative of restitution is, in fact, mythical. As we age and decline, we are never fully restored to how we were before. Such is the way of all things. But isn't it in part true that we all live with a bit of denial, avoiding the painful realities of our own aging? And isn't it true that we have also placed our faith in science and technology to deliver us from it, perhaps to the extent of losing a bit of our own humanity? And the cost has been, too often, prolonged dying experiences and increased suffering. As the bioethicist Daniel Callahan has written, "The greatest success of modern medicine in our lifetime has been to turn former acute causes of death into chronic illnesses"[3]—and it is hurting us in multiple ways. For one, it has increased health care costs exponentially, and forced our society to adopt an insurance scheme that is unjust—today, for instance, there are still twenty-seven million uninsured Americans, a painful reality that

2. Frank, *The Wounded Storyteller.*

3. Callahan, *The Troubled Dream of Life.*

unfortunately reinforces social and economic stratification. But equally important, and too often ignored, is the reality of the toll taken on the patients
themselves, and on their families. Today it is in the news everyday as we
read of the thousands of patients on ventilators in ICUs, of the separation
and isolation, of the unexpected financial costs. And still, we see the denial
and the refusal to engage reality in those who resist getting vaccinated or
wearing masks to protect themselves and their loved ones. The restitution
narrative is too often illusory.

But take away the restitution narrative, that is, provide patients with
just the facts of their conditions without providing them the means to
set those facts in context, and without a reflective process to help them
make meaning and adapt to their circumstances, and we create what Frank
calls the "chaos narrative"[4]—the process of spinning people into fear and
anxiety. We can so easily and unwittingly increase their desperation and,
in turn, deepen the demand on the health care system. While we continue
to make slow progress in helping ill people adapt to their circumstances
resourcefully and creatively, there is still so much more to do. For instance,
we could treat the obesity that leads to diabetes with much better education
so that we could avoid amputations and the disabilities that end up costing
a higher percentage of the health care dollar. We recognize that for those
who have adequate insurance, there is a proportional relationship between
functional decline and cost of health care interventions. As an example,
current explorations into health care costs show us that one third of all
families with a loved one on an ICU in America for longer than two weeks,
will suffer financial hardship. And, when we have the technology available,
we all understand how we tend to feel obligated to use it, not recognizing
that the iatrogenic effects of our high-tech interventions can be as debilitating as the conditions we are attempting to treat. Most of us have faced
horrible scenarios of loved ones in suspended animation, on ventilators, in
acute kidney failure, fighting sepsis, perhaps on paralyzers and amnesiacs,
who then experience a stroke or a bleed in the brain. And we identify with
family members who *never say die*, and whose providers, in desperation,
say "What would you like me to do?", as if now the patient's own thoughts—
arising, remember, out of the *chaos* narrative—should take precedence over
the medical perspective and over our obligation to act in the best interest of
the patient. Against such a scenario we need to learn to say, "Here's what I
recommend, and here is what I am going to do."

4. Frank, *The Wounded Storyteller*.

But there is a third narrative that Frank articulates, which he calls the *quest narrative*,[5] and it is all about the process of meaning-making. The quest narrative invites a process of mutual reflection and exploration. The key is in *how* we create the quest narrative, that is, in how we work with each other and how we work with our patients, so that they stay partners with us in the journey, that is, so they remain collaborative, adaptable, resilient, and able to accept the changing circumstances of their lives. How do we do this? There are a couple of specifics we can utilize.

First, the name of the illness or struggle or condition needs to be taken seriously. And here I am going to reference Margaret Mohrmann, a physician and theologian, writing in one of my ethics textbooks. She says that understanding illness is mostly a matter of getting the description right, and that the description involves far more than the diagnosis[6]. Physicians usually get the diagnosis right, but I can't tell you how often it becomes an unhelpful or meaningless label for the *illness* experienced by the patient, and the number of times I have been with patients when physicians have been present discussing their case, only to turn to me upon the physician's departure and say, "What's a thoracotomy?" "Can you tell me what an AV node is?" "What did he mean by idiopathic cardiomyopathy?" Mohrmann quotes Flannery O'Connor's letters in which she occasionally spoke of the lupus that was her constant companion and that eventually took her life at the age of 39. However, when O'Connor was very anemic, she did not speak of anemia—much less of bone marrow suppression—as her problem, she spoke of *fatigue* and utter exhaustion. A month before her death, when she referred to her illness, she did not mention circulating immune complexes or even nephritis or renal failure. She simply said, "The wolf, I'm afraid, is inside, tearing up the place"[7]. Her experience was not of systemic lupus erythematosus. It was rather her awareness of the chaotic destructive wolf-like gnawing inside that she knew was gradually but inexorably disassembling herself, the term "lupus" coming from the Latin word for wolf.

Mohrmann also references one of John Updike's stories, told by a man who suffered from psoriasis. His description is this: "I am silvery, scaly. Puddles of flakes form wherever I rest my flesh. My torture is skin-deep: there is no pain, not even itching; we lepers live a long time and are ironically healthy in other respects. Lusty, though we are loath to love. Keen-sighted,

5. Frank, *The Wounded Storyteller*.

6. Mohrmann, *Medicine as Ministry*.

7. Mohrmann, *Medicine as Ministry*.

though we hate to look upon ourselves. The name of the disease, spiritually speaking, is humiliation.[8]"

So, it's important to get the diagnosis right: to recognize psoriasis and lupus, cancer and pneumonitis, AIDS and alcoholism, congestive heart failure and mitral valve regurgitation, depression and schizophrenia for what they really are. But secondly, it is no less important, if we want to promote a quest narrative, to get the name of the illness right. It is no less important to recognize that for the sufferer the name of the disease, spiritually speaking, is humiliation, or fear, or malaise, or endless pain, or loneliness, or despair, or the end of a career, or the end of a life. It is no less important to recognize that this is a human being to whom a terrible thing is happening and whatever other name this terrible thing bears its deepest name is *tragedy*.

When we acknowledge the tragedy and give a name to the illness, a name that reflects the experience, the patient responds by beginning the process of meaning-making—the process of reflecting, revaluing their lives, readjusting. It is a quest, to be sure. And when we do so, and when the patient responds, the experience of hospitalization may actually birth a new sense of valuing life. But too often we end up missing the experience and the patient ends up feeling dehumanized. And too many of us end up ourselves feeling less than fulfilled by our vocation and frustrated and despairing in a painful experience of a parallel process.

Once we have provided a name for the illness, the other primary obligation is to listen to the *story* of the patient. Actually, I don't mean listen *to* the story, I mean listen *for* the story. And it is an important distinction. It was Dorothee Soelle who made the important point that there is no freedom from suffering, and that to think that there is, is only a blindness that fails to perceive suffering. "The truth we must hear," she went on to say, "is that we must first *see* the suffering if we are to help relieve it, and we cannot see it without in some sense experiencing it."[9] In fact, to be effective as care providers, requires in some sense that we join in the suffering of the world. And that, in turn, means listening deeply for the story that they have to tell.

I often got called in at the eleventh hour when things had become stuck, and when there was ample alienation among all the parties. Often times the physician and the family were at odds about how to proceed. And when I would ask the patient (if he or she could speak) or the family to tell me their story, what often came up was a litany of loss and fear, a sense

8. Updike, "*The Journal of a Leper.*"
9. Soelle, *The Silent Cry.*

of alienation and of not being heard, a sense that their lives—their whole lives—were coming apart. It is a story of deep and at times indescribable distress. But in the telling of the story, and in the quiet listening, and in the process of remaining present and expressing compassion, hearts begin to soften, and reality begins to take hold, most often accompanied by deep grief. I'd invite you, for instance, to think about how you communicate your thoughts and feelings, about the difference between "giving up" and "letting go," when faced with families who are watching their loved ones die. If implicit in our messages is that they or we ought to hope for miracles or keep up the good fight, we are all caught up in the restitution myth. If explicit in the message is "it may be time to let go and to allow the natural processes of life and of aging to unfold" then we are entering into a quest narrative and resolution can come. It's in the telling of the story that people begin to adapt to change. It is in listening *for* their story and it is in the naming *of* their illness, that we fulfill the primary ethical obligations in the provision of health care.

This is a deeply spiritual process, an opportunity for becoming more spiritually intelligent, more spiritually attuned, more spiritually connected. As such, we do well to refrain from religious language and seek only to stay present, inviting the intimate reflections to come forth. Innocent but ill-advised statements about it being God's will, or about God having a plan, or about God needing another angel in heaven (as was spoken to me following the loss of my son-to-be via miscarriage), or about God's purposes being hidden . . . Such triteness alienates and diminishes, and does nothing to advance meaning-making and spiritual understanding and acceptance. Rather, it is all a part of the inherent suffering of being human and having feelings and struggling to make sense of it all. It is a valiant and beautiful, if also painful and poignant, quest.

Chapter Nine

Creation Spirituality and the Decline of Theism

"Nature is ever at work building and pulling down, creating and destroying, keeping everything whirling and flowing, allowing no rest but in rhythmical motion, chasing everything in endless song out of one beautiful form into another."

—JOHN MUIR, *JOHN MUIR'S CALIFORNIA COLLECTION*

"And the day came when the risk to remain tight in the bud was more painful than the risk it took to blossom."

—ELIZABETH APPELL

IT IS AMAZING TO me how far we have come in thinking about spirituality and spiritual intelligence, and how fast. Even though humans have been deeply spiritual beings since the brain evolved its frontal cortex, the most significant evolution of religion, psychology and spiritual intelligence has happened, really, just over the course of the last hundred years or so, paralleling advances in science and medicine. Stop and think about your own life journeys, about the new insights and perspectives that you have developed as you've read emerging authors and research and conclusions, and as you struggled to make sense of our postmodern, hurting world.

The acceleration in theology really began back in the 1920s with the writings of Albert Schweitzer and Rudolph Bultmann and others who led the way in reforming traditional orthodoxy. But it was in the 50s that things took off, as German and American theologians tried to make sense of things following WW II, and then in the 60s when the Beatles popularized Eastern influences, and when international travel and trade opened everything up. American involvement in Viet Nam and a renewed emphasis on racism and civil rights drove the development in the American consciousness of what was called "the social gospel" (William Sloane Coffin and others), with its emphasis on prophetic engagement and challenging white authoritarian power structures, both in the church and in government. Martin Luther King and James Baldwin and James Cone and Stokely Carmichael and Malcolm X and the Black Panthers all forced traditional religion to examine itself and come to grips with its complicity in oppressing non-whites and the poor. This, in turn, led to the development of "liberation theology," calling into question American imperialism in Central America, the marginalization and brutal oppression of the poor, and the misappropriation of the world's natural resources.

But still, the dominant message remained primarily theistic and evangelical. Carl Barth and Rudolph Bultmann and Paul Tillich were seen as giant intellects and rationalists, on the edges perhaps and held at arms' length, but still considered very much within the tradition, and Wolfhardt Pannenburg and Jurgen Moltmann were the new authoritative voices in religious academia, putting the emphasis on living a life of hope and service in Christ. At the same time, secular expressions of personal liberation were exploding across the counter-culture in what was referred to as the *human potential movement*, with groups such as EST (Erhard Seminars Training) emphasizing "personal responsibility, accountability, and possibility." It was a remarkable time of social awakening, with a significant shadow side. The polarization of American culture seemed to deepen overnight as people, consciously or unconsciously, aligned themselves with one side or the other. Mainstream religious expression got caught in protecting the status quo, while other writers and voices rose up in protest and promoted individual freedom. Just think of the influence of Betty Friedan and Hugh Hefner, of Lenny Bruce and Dick Gregory, of Timothy Leary and Hunter Thompson, of Alan Watts and Ram Dass, of Ken Kesey and Norman Mailer, of Bob Dylan and Janis Joplin. All became "social influencers" and helped shape the rise of social consciousness, while conservative voices such as William

F. Buckley and Billy Graham foreshadowed the Rush Limbaughs and the Tucker Carlsons to come. And the slow polarization of American society and politics had begun.

The mid-twentieth century explosion in theology and psychology seemed to reflect a growing desire for greater meaning and a deeper sense of spirituality for many on the one hand, and drove a sense of anxiety and dread and retrenchment on the other. Boundary breakers vs. the Evangelicals. Trickle-down economics vs. direct aid to the poor. Benevolent authoritarianism vs. "power to the people." MLK vs. Strom Thurmond. Gloria Steinem vs. Phyllis Schlafly. Innovation vs. tradition. Meanwhile, I was being educated to preach meaningfully to the choir and to *preserve* the tradition, and I felt a bit helpless in how to bridge the growing divide, and it was all something of a disconnect to hold at bay in the back of my mind.

It left me wanting for more, so I, like so many of my contemporaries, began to read outside my tradition, latching onto new thinkers and writers in Sojourner's magazine and in Martin Marty's Christian Century and in the more progressive periodicals like the New Yorker and the Atlantic. Thomas Merton was one of those. Merton, who proved to be probably the most influential writer in spirituality from the fifties and sixties, just wasn't on the radar of my tradition, I suppose primarily because he was a Catholic Trappist monk, and a contemplative, something that just didn't fit in mainstream America. And the truth is that those of us preparing for parish ministry in the seventies didn't really read much at all outside of our own narrow traditions and we didn't even *know* about Abraham Joshua Heschel, the great Jewish Rabbi so prophetically involved with the Civil Rights Movement or Teilhard de Chardin, the wonderful French theologian and mystic, or Madeleine L'Engle, who advanced the concepts of Christian universalism and an always-loving, never-judging, divine spirit. The racial unrest and protest movements of the sixties gave rise to new progressive voices which, in turn, shook the theological foundations and the whole process was alive and exciting and in tension, just beginning to open up.

It was a pretty exciting time, and we who were orienting toward the more inclusive and dynamic field of hospital ministry had a sense of being on the edge of something. We were a part of movement, a new way of being in the church, working on the frontiers of medicine and psychology and spirituality. My peers and I knew something exciting was happening, something potentially life-changing and world-shaking. We were the Woodstock generation after all, and if not quite capturing a revolution, it was a significant evolution of social mores and ways of thinking. Long stable traditions were beginning to crumble as experimentation and challenge and new ways of being were coming to the fore. Bob Dylan went electric, public demonstrations became street protests, rock 'n roll intensified, and in light of wars and the nuclear threat and assassinations and climate change, the whole world seemed to be slowly awakening and arising.

In science, Einstein and the astrophysicists and the quantum theorists had opened new vistas, giving rise to new ways of thinking about energy and physical reality and mysticism and spirituality, especially during the fifties, though mostly it was a pretty small circle. But then when Whitehead started talking about "energy" events and divine potentialities, and began to bridge the gap between philosophy and science, those of us who loved theology began to sit up and take notice. And when Jung got the whole therapeutic world talking about the shadow instead of drives, and about dreams and archetypes instead of repression and the id, and about connectedness and universal consciousness instead of compulsive behaviors and arrested development, some new light began to shine on the concepts of original sin and self-worth and hierarchical dominance and the supposed pathways to salvation. The historical-critical method of approaching the scriptures became mandatory in mainstream Christianity and the progressives and the fundamentalists began to widen their differences. Vatican II was held and all of a sudden Catholicism had to wrestle with their own progressive theologians—I remember reading Hans Kung's book entitled *On Being A Christian* at the time, which led to his being defrocked and kicked out of the priesthood.

I love looking at the rapid evolution of thought. By the time I was getting into clinical training, the foundations of Christianity were no longer what we had thought they were. Things were changing rapidly, driven by social and racial unrest. By the late seventies, Transactional Analysis and psychodynamic therapy and the writings of Fritz Perls and Carl Rogers and later Irv Yalom and Rollo May were de rigueur and just giving way to family systems thinking and Murray Bowen and Virginia Satir, and later, Edwin Friedman. And we were doing t-groups and encounter groups and psychodramas and gestalt group processes that generated energy and a strong desire to keep experimenting. There was a sense that consciousness needed to be raised across the board in our culture, and it unfolded in fits and starts, playing out finally in our very professional identities.

We began to recognize that working in hospitals, with broad populations of varying faiths and ethnicities, now rapidly changing due to the explosion in immigration, demanded that we re-brand ourselves, from the term "pastoral" care, which primarily reflected the Christian perspective, to "spiritual" care, a term less aligned with traditional religion. And then it demanded that we engage the very challenging task of defining what we do and establishing standards for how we do it. And that meant defining ourselves, first, as distinct from the tradition and the church, and then *pan*-religiously, as practitioners open to all expressions of spirituality. The question for each of us who were entering into this new field became, "how do I provide meaningful ministry to persons of other faiths or of no faith in a new context and with changing theological and psychological parameters that we can't yet fully grasp?" And the administrators and the doctors and the nurses weren't terribly patient with our parochial ambiguity, basically saying, "if you're going to work here, you need to show up and produce some results." The pressure grew to be *effective*, and to measure outcomes somehow, and a traditional "ministry of presence" characterized by empathic listening, just didn't quite measure up.

At the same time, there was continuous and growing interest in non-traditional spiritual expression. Eastern religious practices grew in their influence, accompanied by the rise of suspect new expressions, the communes and religious cults and the introduction of transcendental meditation. Much of it was exciting and productive; much was frightening and provocative. Clearly, something significant was happening. The ground was shifting, and we were all trying to figure out what the new emphasis on *spirituality* really meant. There were all sorts of varying expressions of it, and God forbid that we might get caught up in the born again movement and/or start talking in tongues or something, but we were in fact recognizing that intellectual discussion of spirituality somehow left us lacking in the ways of living in the spirit, so beautifully described in the scriptures of all major religions. And the values of compassion and loving-kindness (a Buddhist term) and tolerance and inclusion and personal serenity slowing began to rise to the top. Self-help books were proliferating as people everywhere seemed to be struggling to redefine a meaningful personal identity and healthier, more loving relationships and a deepened sense of connection to the divine.

By the mid-eighties, when I was getting into clinical work, there was an explosion of new thought. John Dominic Crossan and Marcus Borg emerged as leaders of the Jesus Project and became prolific writers, reinter-preting the Jesus narrative, daring to question the historicity of the resur-rection story. I was grateful for Borg, and later John Shelby Spong, because in very real ways they saved my rapidly evaporating faith and woke me up to something of far greater meaning and integrity. But it left all of us with a tremendous dilemma. If not "that," then "what?" They were exciting, chal-lenging and demanding days in so many, many ways, trying to write theory papers, trying to figure out where to land, trying to master a new emerging discipline, frankly, trying to just figure out how to "be" given all the rapid influx of new information.

The seventies and eighties also seemed to open up our minds to what was being written about and talked about on TV (thank you Carl Sagan) in science. The moon landing in '69 served as a springboard for both astro-physics and quantum physics, and within a decade theologians within the tradition were writing about what scientific discoveries and theories could mean for personal faith and our understanding of God. Eventually writers like Michael Dowd, the author of *Thank God for Evolution* and a Baptist minister, emerged as spokespersons for a realistic understanding of evolu-tion and the development of the cosmos from the moment of the Big Bang. And feminist writers reinterpreted the patriarchal view of the development of world religions, and of Christianity in particular, from Riane Eisler, au-thor of *The Chalice and the Blade*, to Karen Armstrong, the formerly con-servative Catholic religious sister who wrote prolifically about an inclusive and mystical faith. And following on the heels of Teilhard and L'Engel, writers from Marianne Williamson, the Jewish author who popularized the notion of spiritual transformation and became known as "Oprah's spiritual advisor," to Gary Zukav, the New Age spiritual author who wrote *The Seat of the Soul*, to Wayne Dyer, the internationally renowned writer on self-development—all began to weave together a new way of thinking about spirituality and personal development. And who would have thought that the spiritual leader of Tibet (the Dalai Lama), and a physician born in In-dia (Deepak Chopra), and a neurotic and depressed German-born writer (Eckhardt Tolle) would together become the most influential writers in the new spirituality, opening our horizons to new ways of thinking about re-ligious faith, god images, and self-understanding and our own theological expressions?

Psychology itself was changing, recognizing that the missing piece in the therapeutic process was spirituality and how people made meaning.

The emphasis moved through rational-emotive thought into social psychology, then into transpersonal psychology that began to emphasize the integration of the spiritual and transcendent aspects of the human experience, and then, finally, into a new understanding of and emphasis on consciousness and the internal code of the soul, shaped primarily by James Hillman, reflecting Whitehead's process thought. Hillman, who guided studies at the Carl Jung Institute in Zurich, developed Archetypal Psychology, eventually incorporating the character and calling written deeply into our subconscious and divine nature. It was Sri Aurobindo, the great Indian philosopher-psychologist-scientist who collaborated with Albert Einstein, who first introduced the term "integral psychology" back in the 40's, but then it wasn't for another thirty years until cosmologist and mathematician Ken Wilbur built on Hillman's work and shaped it into what he called the "theory of everything," weaving together concepts of universal consciousness, divine infusion, and psychological development into a holistic world view called Integral Psychology. Phew! Is it any wonder that the term "integration" became the watchword in clinical training to describe the internal process required for practitioners wanting to become nationally certified as spiritual care educators?

Where all this has led for me is into a much more open and wondrous perspective on life and reality. In theology, panentheism became, in fact, the dominant way of understanding life among Christian progressives, defined as God being imbued in all things, as "interpenetrating" everything that is—the God in whom we live and move and have our being, rather than the dualistic sky-God "out there." It builds on the construct that all things are divine, that God is not only in creation but *is* creation itself, that God is indeed the energy of the entire universe, "in, with and under" all things, that God is the essence of everything that is, giving rise to life and unlimited potential as a result. Theism is long gone in progressive thought, and everything we thought before about human expressions of religion has been opened to new ways of thinking and doing and being.

It is as if we humans have come full circle, arriving again where we started, theologically speaking, with a reverence for the earth and the animals, with a feminist embrace of the goddess images of Mother Nature, with a recognition of our place and of the unfolding of the cosmos and of the eternal movement of the divine spirit. We have come to an understanding that all matter is energy, that it changes form constantly, that it dies and is born anew, and that light and energy imbue all things; that everything is in process, that nothing is static (indeed, a new star is born every fifteen seconds, according to the cosmologists), that everything—everything—in all creation, is, in that way, divine. You and me included.

❦ ❦ ❦ ❦ ❦

I got to know Matthew Fox, the foremost writer and spokesperson of what has come to be called Creation Spirituality, while I was working in California, being with him on a couple of different occasions. Fox's journey paralleled the path that so many of us had taken, though he was far more creative and courageous, at least far more than me. He started the Institute of Culture and Creation Spirituality back in 1976, developing what he called an alternative pedagogy to orthodox Catholic theology that would eventually lead to conflict with church authorities and to his expulsion, first from the Dominicans and then from the Catholic Church itself. It was Cardinal Ratzinger who ordered the expulsion for, among other things, refusing to reference God as Father, promoting the concept of Original Blessing over Original Sin, working too closely with Native American spiritual practices, embracing homosexuality, and gradually becoming fully inclusive of other spiritual paths around the world. It all seems to be a fairly moderate expression from our vantage point today, but it really led the evolution of thought in the fields of theology and spirituality at the time. Fox was very influential. It may be a stretch, but it's hard not to think that Ratzinger's heavy handedness (he whom would become Pope Benedict XVI, only to resign some years later) laid the foundation for the very powerful shift in consciousness in the Catholic Church that gave rise to Pope Francis today, a true reformer. Fascinating how the spirit moves in the world!

At its heart, Creation Spirituality embraced all sacred traditions of the late 20th century that were proponents of openness, tolerance and ecological protection. In particular, it came to fully embrace Buddhism, Judaism, Sufism, and Native American spirituality, with a focus on what has come to be called "deep ecumenism." Fox actually built his framework in part on the Middle Ages monk and mystic Meister Eckhart (1260–1328), and utilizes this quote from Eckhart's writing: "Divinity is an underground river that no one can stop, and no one can dam up."[1] Fox wrote about the many different wells that tap into that underground river and stated that it would be wrong to confuse any one well with the flowing of the river itself, that there are many wells that rise into the one river that flows beneath and

---

1. Fox, *Meister Eckhart.*

through and around and in all things. Deep ecumenism teaches that every sacred religious tradition is a wellspring in fact, a bubbling up of the river into the human experience of life-enhancing spirituality; that we best serve the needs of all humanity when we not only respect other religious paths, but collaborate with them in our shared work of healing creation. No one tradition contains all the answers, but every tradition can be (to paraphrase the Buddha) "a finger pointing at the moon," meaning can direct our hearts toward the Source. Notice the metaphors of water, nature and the cosmos.

And it was a perfect fit, I would suggest, for those of us who labored in the field of being hospital chaplains, as we sought to embrace all people, regardless of their spiritual paths or beliefs. "When we learn from and collaborate with fellow-travelers on other spiritual paths," Fox wrote, "our own practices are enriched—and we come one step closer to personal wholeness, and to a world without religious prejudice or fear."[2] Indeed, it began to shape my clinical practice toward defining the purpose or intent of my spiritual care. I came, finally, to this three-fold definition: that we facilitate the adaptation of the patient to their new and frightening reality; that through reflective conversation we assist in the process of meaning making; and that with compassionate engagement and spiritual guidance we generate hope and courage to work through the fear and face an unfolding and uncertain future.

It matters not our previous traditions or personal beliefs; all wells tap into the same river, and all explorations point to the same source. Because we're not focused on the belief system of the patient (or of the student or even of ourselves, as the case may be), we can ground our framework in what may be an emerging universal consciousness around the divine spirit, the earth, and our daily human experience. Creation Spirituality considers itself a "green" theology, emphasizing a holy relationship between humanity and nature, or perhaps better put, an interweaving of life throughout the cosmos. Accordingly, the protection of nature is core, and is considered sacramental even, an expression of the divine and creative spirit and of what Fox calls "the Cosmic Christ," a concept that becomes a transcendent and universal figure of love and the enhancement of life, no longer a "savior" image but an archetype, calling us to become fully human. It has become a theology endorsed by many leading thinkers and artists, among them cultural historian and eco-theologian Thomas Berry, who is a favorite of so many of us. And it's important to

2. Fox, *One River, Many Wells.*

remember that while Fox was coalescing all of this into a definable frame-work, researchers and theorists all around the world were ramping up their studies on climate change and ecology. Not only were we shifting the culture toward heightened awareness of the need to protect and enhance the natural world, but so were we learning about how nature truly functioned, about what was toxic and caused breakdown and, conversely, about what was life-giving and could cause it to thrive. From Rachel Carson's *The Silent Spring* to Berry's works such as *The Sacred Universe* and *The Dream of the Earth* (he is a former Catholic priest as well) to all of the movement toward alternative energy resources and progressive forest management, a huge shift was taking place in eco-consciousness that very much was central to the growing movement in creation spirituality and progressive theological thought.

For instance, we began to recognize that trees are not just essential to life because of their production of oxygen and the lumber they provide, but that they are in fact living organisms that seem to somehow communicate with each other through rhizomes and fungal threads released through their root systems, all in the service of the health and proliferation of the forest. Indeed, every sub-group of trees appears to have a Mother tree that both provides nurturing proteins and pulls back its roots to make space for the young to become more deeply rooted. It is another lovely metaphor, it seems to me, and a lesson in why clear-cutting forests doesn't allow for regeneration the way selective cutting does. Norway, in fact, just recently became the first country to totally ban deforestation. When we walk in the woods, we might be mindful of the sacredness of all that is around us—the wisdom and nurture of the mother trees, the creative energy embedded in the rocks, the vitality and life-giving force of the water. As the wave is in the lake, so is God in all things, ever moving, ever creating, ever renewing.

Fox is actually more of an interpreter of the evolution of thought in postmodern spirituality than he is a theorist, and his great gift, it seems to me, is summarizing and popularizing the writings of so many others. Drawing on a spirituality of "original blessing" (rather than the traditional theological concept of "original sin") we might say that all that *is*, is good and filled with potential, that all of life and creation is sacred and a mani-festation of beauty and delight. This is core creation spirituality which, according to Fox, has these hallmarks:

- it is a marriage of spirituality, science and creativity (as we learn, so do we grow; as we engage the processes of creation, so do we deepen spiritually);

- it is an *embodied* spirituality, meaning that it invites us to use our minds, our bodies, our perceptions, our senses and our feelings in all forms of interaction, always inviting expressions of love and connection;

- it is a *universal* spirituality that is given expression in hymns and psalms and gospels and chants and sacred circle dances and dharma teachings and incantations and meditations and devotions and sweat lodges and sacraments and prayers of all traditions throughout all the nations of the world;

- and it is an *interconnected* spirituality, recognizing that as one does better, we all do better, that compassion and joy rise up in us as we become conscious of each other's needs and appreciative of the full spectrum of diversity, always mindful of working for justice and fullness of life for each other as well as for ourselves.[3]

Thomas Merton famously proposed a four-fold path of spiritual practice, which has been reinterpreted and restated many times over the years by various authors. I find it helpful to have such a framework, since spiritual practice is all about being intentional in moving toward a fuller experience of the divine. That, by the way, is not something that was taught in my tradition or in the seminary, or maybe I just missed it. "Experiencing" God just wasn't very Lutheran or Scandinavian, if you will. We even held suspect those who did. And you may all identify somewhat with my experience that worship and prayer and devotional reading were always far more about living rightly and with a certain sense of piety than they were about connecting with the sacred. That may explain why such things as meditation and introspective reflection and learning about other faith traditions were not a part of the mainstream evangelical tradition. How things have changed! Today, it seems, we all thirst for greater awareness and consciousness, of divine movement in the world in general, and in our daily lives in particular. Here is a way to think about a four-fold path of spiritual practice as a way of doing exactly that, of experiencing the divine, which is found in the in-and-out flow between these following expressions:

3. Fox, *Original Blessing.*

- Firstly, *the path of awe*: raising our awareness, becoming attuned to the unfolding of the miraculous and wonderful all around us, seeking out beauty and joy and wonder and amazement. The path of awe is about recognizing and embracing the sacred embedded in all of creation and in the depth and mystery of one another, and letting its beauty and awesomeness bubble up like a refreshing fountain, sometimes just overwhelming us!

- Secondly, *the path of release*: the spiritual journey emphasizes the depths of things, with themes of embracing the human condition, the brokenness, the sorrows of life, the pain and suffering. In making space for the depths, we are invited toward a certain reorientation that calls us to let go and let be, and to embrace both our powerlessness and our unlimited potential. As healers, we start with radical acceptance, with creating the holding space, where the light can begin to enter the darkness. So—what do you need to let go of? What pain and sadness or even dysfunction might you release and turn over? I like the concept here of traveling lightly, of letting go of the things that burden us and weigh us down. And I recognize that it's not always an easy path to follow.

- Then third, *the path of creativity*: this is the focus on being generative, borrowing Whitehead's sense that we are co-creators with God. Can we trust the images and senses and feelings and moments of insight and clarity that come to us from outside or that bubble up within us from the wellsprings of the divine river? God knows all potentialities and provides an inrush of data, Whitehead wrote, inviting heightened awareness and greater choice as we birth new ways of being into existence.

- And finally, *the path of transformation*. When we are generative and creative, new opportunities, thoughts and ideas emerge in our thinking and in our lives, new people and new experiences come, and we are opened to new ways of being. When you follow your bliss, Joseph Campbell wrote, new transformative experiences come to you. Individual transformation is a process that unfolds as we raise our consciousness (the pathway of awe) and let go of what is stopping us up (the pathway of release), and as we engage what is unfolding within and in front of us (the pathway of creativity). And inevitably we become drawn to advocacy work, to the work of compassion, to the work of justice and love for others (the path of transformation), because we are experiencing renewal ourselves.

So, in creation spirituality, we are all mystics and we are all prophets and we are all filled with the potential to become and embody more than we have been. For our purposes here, this serves as in invitation first to let go of cynicism, painful memories, resentments, internalized bad feelings and self-limiting thinking, and then to embrace the potential of the present moment, the unfolding of God's generative energy, deepening and broadening and expanding our lives, indeed trusting the process of transformation and becoming. As it is written, "Behold, I make all things new!"

Fritjof Capra, the great physicist, contributed to the development of Creation Spirituality as well, coming at it from the perspective of science. Capra, you may know, is also an educator and a systems theorist, who worked for many years at CERN, the European Organization for Nuclear Research in Switzerland. His first major written work was entitled *The Tao of Physics*, which indicated that he likes to write about the crossroads or interweaving of science and spirituality. His most recent book, entitled *The Systems View of Life*, integrates the biological, cognitive, social and ecological dimensions of life into one unified vision. He notes that science has discovered that the material world, ultimately—and the whole cosmos for that matter—is a network of inseparable patterns of relationships; indeed, that our planet is a "living, self-regulating system of interacting sub-systems and relationships."[4] The same is true for the human body. The body and mind are not separate but fully integrated with one another; the brain and the immune system and our bodily organs and even every single cell are an expression of living, cognitive systems, and he puts his emphases on complexity, nonlinearity, and the incredibly beautiful systems of organization that each of us carries.

Spirituality, for Capra, is a direct, non-intellectual experience of reality during moments of "heightened aliveness," when all the systems are interacting fully. Abraham Maslow, the human motivation psychologist, described that as a "peak experience;" Buddhists refer to it as the fullest expression of "mindfulness;" other writers as "fullness of mind and body" or as being "in flow." A spiritual experience, according to Capra, is always embodied, that is, it is an experience of aliveness of mind and body as a unity which transcends not only our tendency to see them as separate, but

4. Capra & Luisi, *System Views of Life*.

transcends the separation of self and world and of self and God. It generates a profound sense of "oneness" with all things, and a profound sense of
belonging to the universe as a whole.

This sense of belonging, combined with the senses of awe and wonder
and humility—all stemming from an encounter with mystery, from a "waking up" to a reality that is ineffable, that is undefinable and totally mysterious—are what make up or define "spirituality" for Capra, and I think that is
beautifully put. And it is the highest form of evolution. He notes that to get
here, we went through a long process of evolution, from the first organizing
vesicles of water chemicals to the first bacterial cell, to all the life forms that
followed. But what is unique in this perspective, now becoming dominant
in scientific thinking, is that in the majestic unfolding of life, all living organisms continually respond to environmental influences with structural
changes that are arrived at autonomously, according to their own complex
internal systems. Over the course of history, each strand of creation developed its own complexity. But as their structures increased in complexity
so did their so-called "cognitive" processes, eventually bringing forth the
shared conscious awareness and language and conceptual thought that we
all now describe as the universe becoming conscious of itself.

For all of this to happen, every autonomous system had to figure out
a way to communicate with and interact with other systems, first within
each organism and then between each organism, creating in fact new and
more complex systems, with each organism in turn learning and growing
accordingly. And the outstanding characteristic of the highest non-animal
system with which we are familiar—the earth itself—is its inherent ability
to generate and sustain life. The earth developed its own capacity to make
life possible, and not just basic life, but life that finally recognizes itself as
sacred and as an expression of the divine. The earth made itself conscious
of itself, through *us*, through we who are of the earth. When we are truly
awakened to that fact, then all subsystems become indispensable, essential
to the process, truly holy, in fact. And our spiritual obligation, as embodi-
ments of the universe's consciousness, becomes, obviously, to protect and
enhance our environment and one another.

This is true *creation spirituality*, with its emphasis on deep ecology, on
connectedness, relationship, interdependence and belonging. The defining
characteristic of all of this is something of a paradigm shift from anthro-
pocentric to eco-centric values. It is a worldview that acknowledges the
inherent value of non-human life, of embedded energy, of hidden potential,

and of the process of becoming for all, recognizing that all living beings are members of ecological and spiritual communities, bound together as networks of interdependencies.

One other piece here: insightful, brilliant people throughout human history, people like the ancient Chinese, the Sufis, the Egyptians, and such luminaries as Pythagoras in ancient Greece and Galileo and Kepler in Europe, all recognized what we have come to call Sacred Geometry, the mathematical formulas and patterns that appear throughout nature, throughout the cosmos in fact, and are now confirmed to exist throughout the quantum world as well. From DaVinci's Vitruvian Man to the Golden Ratio to the Flower of Life to the patterns of sacred geometry in harmonics to Spiral Dynamics and the wonder of fractals (repeating geometric patterns in any one organism through progressively smaller dimensions), what we see today is a consistent, harmonious, and progressive expression of creation. But more than just something reducible to intellectual observation, what we see is beautiful, an expression of something more than itself, an expression of what can only be described as divine.

When we look at the world around us, the trees and the rocks and the waters and one another, we find that we are not thrown into chaos and randomness, as so many want to cast the process of evolution, but we are a part of a great order, a grand symphony of life. Every molecule in our bodies was once a part of previous bodies, living or nonliving, and will be a part of future bodies, and every molecule reflects not only beauty but the potential for new life once more. In this sense our body doesn't disappear when we die, but transforms, living on, again and again, as the atoms and molecules become again something new, because life itself lives on. And perhaps more significantly, that which orders our own individual systems in our own bodies, can only be called eternal as well, whether we understand it as soul or spirit or energy or God or what have you; it is both wholly embodied and wholly without, "the whence and the whither," to quote the guy who turned me on to all of this in the first place, my favorite professor, Paul Sponheim.[5] It may be both something of which we are conscious (it appears that indeed we can influence our reality simply by being intentional about envisioning it) and something which moves forward whether we are conscious of it or not, something of which we can barely grasp. Our concepts and metaphors are embedded in the web of life, together with our bodies, our brains, our minds, and our world. Indeed, we belong to the universe, and

5. Sponheim, *God, the Whence and the Whither.*

this experience of belonging, the height of our spirituality, makes our lives profoundly rich and profoundly meaningful.

Still, our reluctance to honor the spirituality of creation itself, of Mother Nature, of our world, suggests that we are "sleepwalking toward the edge of a cliff," as the scientists say, failing somehow in our awareness, as if we don't care. Climate activists and environmentalists seem to be slamming their heads against a wall, trying to heighten our awareness of the gravity of our situation. But being mindful of trying to maintain an intelligent spiritual perspective, we recognize it isn't global warming and environmental degradation that are the source problems, it is something far more human. Gus Speth, the founder of the National Resources Defense Council, perhaps said it best: "I used to think that the top environmental problems were biodiversity loss, ecosystem collapse, and climate change. I thought that thirty years of good science could address these problems. I was wrong. The top environmental problems are selfishness, greed, and apathy. And to deal with these we need a cultural and spiritual transformation. And we scientists don't know how to do that."[6]

Alienation from nature, together with the loss of the experience of being a part of the living creation of planet Earth, may be the greatest tragedy of the materialistic era. It is in fact *the* causative reason for ecological disaster and climate change. Far from the evangelical tradition of humankind being masters of nature and having "dominion" over all the creatures and resources of the world, we recognize that mistreating Mother Nature—as we are certainly doing, in the extreme—is tantamount to suicide, not dominion. And we are all in this together, we are all culpable. Therefore, to open our future to possibility once again, we need to change our consciousness, our spirituality, our mindset. We need, if not a new religion, then an awakening to a new, collaborative, committed and intertwined spirituality of gratitude.

Richard Rohr writes: "Healthy religion names what is real, what's true, what really works, what works in the long run—both now and later. This ultimate reality—the ways things really work—is quite simply described as love. It is all, simply, an expression of God's love. And religion at its best teaches us that way of love." Creation Spirituality is, ultimately, simply embracing that love, walking in the way of that love, and expressing that love in all things—a transcendent, transformative and generative way of being.

---

6. Speth, *"Gus Speth Calls for a 'New Environmentalism'".*

As the wonderful poet Mary Oliver so beautifully summarized, "My work is *loving* the world."[7]

7. Oliver, "*The Messenger*," 1.

Chapter Ten

Evolutionary Spirituality and the New Universe Story

"The first peace, which is the most important, is that which comes within the souls of men and women when they realize their relationship, their oneness with the Universe and all its powers."

—BLACK ELK, LAKOTA ELDER AND TEACHER,
BLACK ELK SPEAKS

I WAS AT CONFIRMATION camp in northern Minnesota, one beautiful summer week when I was fourteen years old. Being in the boreal forest, on the shore of a gorgeous lake, I felt alive and engaged. Something was happening. I certainly didn't understand it all at the time, but it was clearly hormonal, and intellectual, and profoundly spiritual, and I had the sense that things were beginning to coalesce in my life, that I was in a very stimulating process of becoming. I just didn't have a clue about what that was to be. I was tentative and anxious, I was curious and fascinated, all at the same time, in both my body and spirit. There were kids from several other church youth groups in camp with us, and we were all mixed together in our cabins and activities and learning groups.

One of them, cute and vivacious and fun, was named Colleen. We were clearly attracted to each other, but I was also intimidated, having no clue what to do with such strange and new feelings. On the last night of camp, just after dusk, she ran over to me and took my hand and asked me to go for a walk through the meadow with her. I was somewhat undone, a bit naïve, and yet I wanted to respond to the affirmation and connection. I noticed a few other couples doing the same thing and, well, off we went, with my heart thumping in my chest. When we came near to the far edge of the meadow, she asked me to sit down with her in the soft grass and then to lay down and look up at the sky. And I did, in a way I had never done before. But it wasn't what I anticipated. Rather than talking about the week together or slowly making physical advances, she started pointing out the planets and the constellations that were shining so clearly on that glorious night, telling me of their mythological significance, expressing freely her awe and wonder as she did so. The whole Milky Way just spread out before us. It was disarming—and overwhelming. And it became something of a numinous moment for me. All my feelings of self-doubt—and of arousal— dissipated as we both got lost in the incredible beauty and mystery of the cosmos. It felt sacred somehow, humbling and quieting.

We talked comfortably about what we thought God really was, about what might happen in our lives to come, about how good it felt to be in that place at that moment. We ooh-ed and aah-ed at the occasional shoot-ing star and were fascinated by the fireflies flitting about, getting the sense that we were a part of the heavens, not separate from them. It was the first time I had ever been truly intimate with another person outside my fam-ily—certainly never with a girl!—and it had the effect of calming me, and my anxiety subsided, and I felt strangely contented and joyful, and my world opened up, just like that. It was my first true spiritual experience, as everything around me seemed to glow in a kind of radiance and as I felt transported, becoming at one with the universe. After that forty-five minutes or so, she leaned over, kissed me on the cheek, thanked me for being with her, grabbed my hand again, and off we went back to join the others at the campfire. And my awe at the cosmos, and my sense of place in things, has never left me. What a gift she was to me. Here is the story of what we were looking at:

It was approximately fourteen billion years ago, from the restless emptiness of quantum space, that a creative energy exploded into being, bearing all matter, all dimension, all possibility, and all time. The tempera-ture exceeded one trillion degrees centigrade, instantly cooling to produce the first elementary particles: electrons, protons and neutrons, all shooting forth to seed the vastness. The paradox of creation and destruction amidst the cosmic dust that filled the vacuum of space began to shape the evolving rhythms and patterns of the rapidly-expanding new universe. Chaotic and destructive and generative, creation's paradoxical wisdom began to coalesce. By ten billion years ago, the first stars began to illuminate the darkness, many of them intensely hot. They flared up and exploded in brilliant supernovas, each as bright as an entire galaxy, spewing off creative gases and energies and generating new stars as they did so. The cycle of birth, death and rebirth became the inspiring process that would endow creation for time immemorial. The force of those explosions sent heavier elements hurtling through space, condensing into still more new stars in the far reaches of the cosmos, where the process continued on and on.

By about 4.5 billion years ago, the process we refer to as *cosmogenesis* irrupted in a new range of supernova explosions releasing spiraling clouds of gas, generating new suns and solar systems and galaxies throughout the void, with stars now beginning to be in relationship with one another, fed and connected by millions of suns. One spiral in this new irruption, what we came to call the Milky Way, was to become home to our sun and to the many stars that illuminate our night skies. Born out of an explosion of 10,000 stars all at once, with a volume one million times that of our earth, the sun exerted its influence on complex molecules within its sphere of influence, and endowed the emerging planets around it with a creative balance of gravitational and electromagnetic forces. By 3.8 billion years ago, our home planet, the earth, began to take shape. Uniquely poised relative to the sun's influence on it, earth brought forth cosmogenetic powers unknown in any other region of creation. By 3.5 billion years ago, the rich array of cosmic liquids and chemicals formed yet another new alliance, birthing forth the earliest life-forms: tiny bacteria that thrive even to our current time. Meanwhile our sun was stimulating a startlingly new and uniquely different process of creation. Through the process of photosynthesis referenced earlier, the sun's energy began to stimulate the growth of green plants, which in turn absorbed the toxic CO_2 in the atmosphere and converted it into oxygen, and life in all its varied and amazing iterations, began. The sun seemingly created and then entered into the food-chain, gracing every organism with nurturing abundance and unlimited potential.

Then, 350 million years ago, with flowers adorning the landscape, and trees towering above the earth's crust and with fish abounding in the waters, sea mammals began to move onto the land, and the complexity of embodied life reached a new apex of elegance and beauty as the myriad animal species began to proliferate, ever growing, ever changing, ever evolving. By seven million years ago, bi-ped animals, with growing brains, emerged in Africa, eventually giving rise to human species just some 200,000 to 300,000 years ago. Evolving and learning and developing skills, several human species flourished and competed for dominance, with our own, Homo Sapiens, eventually moving out of Africa to inhabit the entire planet, bringing forth new mental and physical and spiritual powers. We can say now that this creative process was the way in which the universe eventually became conscious of itself, as we look out at the stars and ponder our place, still struggling to make sense of our awesome existence.

Perhaps the zenith of this story is to note that it was just 52 years ago that we humans visited another celestial body for the first time. Glancing back from their base on the moon, humans saw the earth as a blue-white pearl, illuminated by the sun. This iconic image has changed our perceptions forever, inviting us to see anew our place as cosmic-planetary creatures who live because of the sun's beautiful warmth and light and energy, and whose essential vocation is to treat all of creation with the reverence and care it deserves. Brian Swimme, the brilliant cosmologist and writer, has stated it so beautifully:

> In the case of the Sun, we have a new understanding of the cosmological meaning of sacrifice. The Sun is, with each second, transforming four million tons of itself into light— giving itself over to become energy that we, with every meal, partake of. The Sun converts itself into a flow of energy that through photosynthesis, changes into plants that are then consumed by animals. Humans have been feasting on the Sun's energy, stored in the form of wheat or maize or reindeer forever, as each day the Sun dies a little bit more and is reborn again as the vitality of Earth. These solar flares are in fact the very power of the vast human enterprise. Every child of ours needs to learn the simple truth: she is the energy of the Sun. And we adults should organize things so her face shines with the same radiant joy.[1]

> —Brian Swimme

What an awesome story this is. Today, when I stand and gaze at the night sky, I remain fascinated and overwhelmed and powerfully humbled. Like every person before me, we wonder how this happened, what put it in motion, how and why it continues to unfold in ever more complex and beautiful ways. To become spiritually intelligent is to, among everything

1. Swimme, *The Hidden Heart of the Cosmos*, 40–41.

else, honor and acknowledge and ponder the continually evolving creative process. Like the fourteen-year-old boy at bible camp, I wonder still about the nature of the divine mystery that imbues the universe with such creative energy, and the earth with such incredible life. I am most often left speechless. But there are some things we can say, now gathered under the term "evolutionary spirituality," and they are these:

- Evolutionary spirituality (ES) is about learning to be in right relationship with the reality of a continually unfolding and dynamic universe, and about grounding ourselves in the interconnected processes of growth and continual unfolding of becoming more than we are. Acceptance, trust, perspective, and faith all flow out of living into that unfolding. Because we are interconnected, when we are not aligned with that reality, we suffer, and so do those around us. Evolutionary spirituality embraces practices that can help us find and create such alignment. When we align with the potential of evolving possibility, we thrive. When we deny it or resist it or fight against it, we constrict, we curve inward, we seed the potential for hurt and pain and separateness. It is folly to attempt to maintain things as they are, whether we are talking about religious beliefs or relationships or political alliances. Energy is always dynamic; we are ever-changing. Life is an unfolding journey. Perhaps our primary task is to enjoy the ride and learn as we go.

- It is through an evolutionary calling that we come into right relationship with the future. That evolutionary calling is toward the paths of action in the world where your joys and gifts intersect with the world's needs. This requires integration and openness, now most often referred to as "deep integrity." To have deep integrity is to love the unfolding and all that is within it.

- By engaging in practices that move us along the path of deep integrity, we discover that humility, trust, authenticity, responsibility and service (the five character traits of deep integrity) emerge naturally within and through us. The cleaning up of character—this unmasking of hidden potential—is indeed the reason that all the world's spiritual practices evolved. Deep integrity offers the promise of meaningful connection with the divine, through our openness, our perceptivity, our awe and our wonder. And the freedom we discover clears us to devote our energies toward evolutionary ends, that is, toward greater possibility and becoming, which is the pathway toward personal fulfillment.

- Evolutionary impulses manifest most powerfully in collaboration with others; the flow is so much bigger than any of our individual perspectives. Consciousness itself, along with intuition and the physical senses, is evolving as well. We do not know what the future holds, but we know the process itself is creative and expansive and results in wonderful things.

- Collective learning is accelerating, as technology evolves and expands. As human communities and networks connect us up while continuing to evolve, inner transformation is accelerated. Through a process of fits and starts, of quantum leaps forward and small steps backward, we are becoming more than we have been, and it is happening faster than ever.

- The practices for coming into right relationship with reality and with the divine spirit are drawn from spiritual practices old and new. They foster mystical experiences and integral thinking— that all things in the universe are connected. They embrace the most life-affirming wisdom and tools from all of humanity's spiritual and religious heritage by deepening meaning-making processes through the integration of theology with evolutionary and cosmological science. There is no going back. The wisdom of our religious traditions is not something only to be preserved; indeed, it is a profound resource for entering into the newness of an unknown future with faith and trust and courage.

- Evolutionary spirituality acknowledges the "evolutionary impulse" that drives the entire cosmos and that is reflective of and grounded in the divine, in what may be called the Source, the Ground of All Being, the Spirit, or God. That energy that permeates you and I as well as the entire universe is creative and life-giving and amazing!

- We hold that the mystery of the divine spirit, the source of all things, is imbued in the authentic self of each person and that every person and everything in the cosmos is an expression of the divine; that the divine is what generates potential and creativity, including the potential for collective intelligence, consciousness, and continuing evolution toward still greater complexity and beauty.

- ES asserts that the interior realm of consciousness evolves in concert with the exterior realm of matter as we learn more about it, that it is directly manifested in human consciousness and culture, and is developmental and progressive, and evolves from egocentricity to ethnocentricity to worldcentricity to cosmocentricity. Our scope includes all that is, seen and unseen.

- ES recognizes that individual spiritual transformation is essential for cultural evolution. We co-create the "coming into being" of the future with intentional learning and reorientation.

- We are indeed the universe becoming conscious of itself. Evolutionary spirituality combines spiritual and scientific insights to create a comprehensive understanding of humanity and the universe, recognizing that human beings today are at the leading edge of that fourteen billion year evolutionary process that originated with the Big Bang, and that humanity's emerging awareness of this process has profound philosophical and spiritual implications.

- We embrace progressive evolutionary science and the newest discoveries of cosmology, astrophysics, and quantum physics, while promoting universal and deep spiritual, ethical and moral leverage and legitimacy. It is that legitimacy that compels us and motivates us toward personal and communal growth while supporting empowerment and vitality for global sustainability, deep ecology, and environmentalism.

This perspective gives credence to saying that we are, indeed, in God and that God is, indeed, in us; that we are, in fact, an essential part of the divine unfolding. We wrestle so much with a sense of alienation and isolation in contemporary life, but this reframes everything. Given what we are learning about interconnectedness and quantum energy, we might say that we can never be separated from the divine because we are a living and loving *expression* of the divine; we might even say that we are an extension of the divine spirit, the means through which the divine spirit is given consciousness and community and creativity and love.

Our struggle plays out by keeping our perspectives too narrow and our reflections too small. As we live into and embrace evolutionary spirituality, we open ourselves to a future of loving and compassionate connection with one another. Political and cultural differences recede in both importance and effect. Awe and wonder become the defining characteristics of a spirit-consciousness community, and deep integrity becomes the order of the day as we come to recognize our interconnectedness and our oneness. As the wonderful cosmologist Neil deGrasse Tyson has stated, "we are all connected to each other biologically, to the earth chemically and to the rest of the universe atomically . . . . We are in the universe, and the universe is in us."[2]

2. Tyson, "*The Universe.*"

Chapter Eleven

Mysticism, Spiritual Experiences and the Collective Unconscious

"The task of religion is not to turn us into proper believers; it is to deepen the personal within us, to embrace the power of life, to expand our consciousness, in order that we might see things that eyes do not normally see."

—JOHN SHELBY SPONG, *ETERNAL LIFE: A NEW VISION*

WHEN I WAS THAT fourteen-year-old boy at confirmation camp, I had no clue what the term "mysticism" meant, or what a mystical or spiritual experience might be. Nonetheless, I knew that something out-of-the-ordinary had happened that evening, and that it was uniquely meaningful. I have had several other similar experiences over the years, usually during a time of sorrow or stress or, conversely, of joy and happiness. Perhaps they were moments of heightened consciousness or peak experiences welling up from within, although they always felt like something coming into me from outside of me, something enhancing the moment, loving me through whatever I was experiencing.

When I was a brand new parish minister, after having my self-esteem shaken in early clinical training, I was quite anxious about public speaking (not a good thing for a minister!) and I found it difficult to handle the internal pressure. One of my first sermons was to be preached for a major church festival, and the church was packed. The senior minister had a somewhat remote and critical personality and added to my anxiety by silently conveying his scrutiny. I had carefully prepared my message, had it memorized, and knew that it would be well received; still, my anxiety continued to rise, so that when I stepped into the pulpit, I had difficulty breathing and speaking. Making it worse, I knew, of course, that it was obvious to all. But then, just as I was reaching the edge of panic, I felt a hand being gently and warmly placed on my shoulder, and the message was clear: "you are not alone, I am with you, you'll be okay, you can do this." I paused, I quieted down, my confidence returned, and I proceeded to present my homily. For the rest of the service the sanctuary seemed to be bathed in something of a golden light, softly glowing, lovely. The experience was very real to me and it left me awed and humbled and not a little undone. I could literally feel each of the fingers and the thumb there on my shoulder, I could feel the warmth and the care, I could sense the presence. Might it have been my grandfather who had just recently died, I wondered? Might it have been—dare I say it—Jesus? Over the years, I felt that presence again several times. And whenever I shared my story with friends and students, I was always struck by how many had had similar experiences, and like me, had no clue about what to make of them.

Its challenging to write about spiritual experiences in a cogent way; they lie outside of normal experience, even outside of our normative understanding of reality. Still, they are far from uncommon. As a chaplain, I heard dozens of stories from patients and their families of near-death spiritual experiences. It was not at all uncommon to be in the room when someone was dying when their body would relax, when their face would soften, when a smile would come to their lips at just the moment before death. One older gentleman, who had been unresponsive for a couple of days, stirred gently, opened his eyes, seemed to look about the empty room behind me with a warm and loving smile, whispered "I love you all!" and slipped away. Some patients survived such moments and couldn't wait to tell me about them, about whom they saw, about being out of their bodies and more aware of things than ever before, about the passageway of light, about loved ones waiting for them "on the other side," about spiritual beings coming to them, filling the room with a sense of sacred love. Such moments were profoundly significant for so many.

I don't know Anita Moorjani, but I have followed her and read her posts on social media. Her story seems particularly relevant to these reflections. She was at the end stage of cancer, and her organs were slowly shutting down. She had lost nearly a quarter of her body weight, and with it the last vestiges of her vitality, and she eventually became somnolent and mostly unresponsive, now under in-patient hospice care. She had multiple tumors in her lymphatic system, she was unable to clear the accumulating fluid in her lungs, she was in and out of consciousness, and her breathing was erratic and labored. It was clear that death was near. She was only forty-six. Anita was one who dramatically survived her near death experience, and who went on recover, as her cancer receded, over time becoming a nearly insignificant chronic illness. This is what she experienced, in her own words:

> In the near-death state, I was more acutely aware of all that was going on than I've ever been in a normal physical state. I wasn't using my five biological senses, yet I was keenly taking everything in. It was as though another, completely different type of perception kicked in, and more than just perceive, I seemed to also encompass everything that was happening, as though I was slowly merging with it all. I knew when people came in to see me, who they were and what they were doing, although my physical eyes were closed. The sharpness of my perception was more intense than if I'd been using my physical senses. I seemed to just know and understand everything—not only what was going on around me, but also what everyone was feeling, as though I was able to see and feel through each person. I was extremely aware of every detail, but I couldn't physically feel anything—except a release and a level of freedom I'd never known before. I felt no emotional attachment to my body. I felt free, liberated and magnificent. Every pain, ache, sadness, and sorrow was gone. I began to feel weightless and to become aware that I was able to be anywhere at any time . . . and this didn't seem unusual. It felt normal, as though this were the real way to perceive things.
>
> I was fully aware of every word of the conversation that was taking place between my family and the doctors, although it was physically some distance away, outside my room. I saw the frightened expression on my husband's face and could feel his fear. It was as though, in that instant, I became him. Simultaneously, I became aware that my brother was thousands of miles away on an airplane, coming to see me. I saw him and his worried look. Each time my emotions took over the situation and I felt myself being drawn into the drama of the physical realm, I discovered myself starting to expand again, and I felt a release from all attachment.

I felt a sense of freedom and liberation that I'd never experienced in my physical life before. I can only describe this as the combination of joy mixed with a generous sprinkling of jubilation and happiness. A superb and glorious unconditional love surrounded me, wrapping me tight as I continued to let go. I didn't feel as though I'd physically gone somewhere else—it was more as though I'd awakened. My consciousness was finally realizing its true magnificence and in doing so, it was expanding beyond my body and this physical world, until it encompassed not only this existence, but continued to expand into another realm that was beyond time and space, and at the same time included it. Love, joy, ecstasy and awe poured into me, through me, and engulfed me. I was swallowed up and enveloped in more love than I ever knew existed. I felt more free and alive than I ever had.

The feeling of complete, pure, unconditional love was unlike anything I'd known before. To my amazement, I became aware of the presence of my father, who'd died ten years earlier. There were no words, but I clearly understood. And then I recognized the essence of my best friend, Susan, who had died three years prior. I felt what I can only describe as excitement as their presence enveloped me like a warm embrace, and I was comforted. I was also aware of other beings around me. I didn't recognize them, but I knew they loved me very much. It was tremendously comforting for me to reconnect with Susan's essence. I felt nothing but unconditional love, both from her and for her. And then, just as I experienced that, I understood that she was here, there, and everywhere. She was able to be in all places at all times for all her loved ones.

Although I was no longer using my five physical senses, I had unlimited perception, as if a new sense had become available, one that was more heightened than any of our usual faculties. I had 360-degree peripheral vision with total awareness of my surroundings. And as amazing as it all sounds, it still felt almost normal. Time felt different in that realm, too, and I felt all moments at once. My awareness in that expanded realm was indescribable, despite my best efforts to explain it. The clarity was amazing. In that state of clarity, I also realized that I'm not who I'd always thought I was: Here I am without my body, race, culture, religion, or beliefs . . . yet I continue to exist. I certainly didn't feel reduced or smaller in any way. On the contrary, I hadn't ever been this huge, this powerful, or this all-encompassing. I felt eternal, as if I'd always existed and always would without beginning or end. The understanding was so clear: I was looking into a new paradigm of self, becoming the crystalline light of my own awareness. Nothing interfered with the flow, glory, and amazing beauty of what was taking place. I realized that the entire universe is alive and infused with consciousness, encompassing all of life and nature. We're all facets of that Unity—we're all One. It was as though I was enveloped in the oneness, the pure essence of every living being, without their pains, dramas, and egos. I understood that at the core, our essence is made of pure love. We are pure love—every single one of us.[1]

❊ ❊ ❊ ❊ ❊

It became clear to me early on in my career, that there was so much going on that I just didn't understand, that I was unable to perceive or fully grasp. Could it be that our consciousness was limited by our own narrow self-understanding? Was there really another "plane of existence" for lack of a better term, that we just weren't developed enough to access? The "breaking-in" of the Holy Spirit was a time-honored phrase in our religious traditions, but what was that really referring to? Was there indeed a divine source, a divine spirit that was engaged with us, that came to us, that opened us up and awakened us to a deeper, or higher, reality, that actually provided perspective to help us cope with the pain of life, to even, in fact, turn things around for us? In my moments of quiet reflection, I would wonder and ponder, like so many before me, who or what it was that was really looking out through my eyes. Clearly, I was more than my body. You may all be familiar with the quote attributed to C.S. Lewis (though it is likely not authentic to him) who stated, "You don't have a soul, you *are* a soul; you *have* a body." Since there is no "center" to the brain, and since consciousness seems more to be something we tap into rather than something we strictly generate in our bodies, could it be that that which animates us and inspires us and stimulates our creativity is something *more* than us? And if we are something more than our bodies, the ramifications are endless and even mind-blowing.

William James, the hugely influential pragmatic philosopher and psychologist of the late 19th and early 20th centuries, took on this mystery in his *Varieties of Religious Experience*, published in 1902. Based on his study of accounts of mystical experiences, he concluded that such experiences tend to contain two primary features, *illumination* and *union*[2]. His term "illumination" had double meaning: the experiences usually involved a quality of luminosity or radiance, and led to an experience of "enlightenment,"

1. Moorjani, *Dying To Be Me*.
2. James, *Varieties of Religious Experience*, 16, 92.

that is, to a new way of seeing, a new sense of understanding. The term "union" referred to the sense of connectedness to the divine that so many people reported, the disappearance or softening of the boundaries between the self and all else. Such experiences almost always led to a shift in perspective, to a new way of seeing, a changed orientation to finding joy and meaning in life.

James noted other common qualities of spiritual experiences as well. He described them this way: *ineffability*, the inability to put such overwhelming experiences into meaningful words; *transiency*, they tend to be brief and to come and go; *passivity*, meaning that we can't make them happen, they happen *to* us, they come into us from outside or, perhaps, from deep within; and they have a *noetic quality*, meaning they include a vivid sense of knowing, a strong sense of seeing more clearly and with greater certainty than ever before.

Rudolph Otto, the great German theologian and scholar, referred to spiritual experiences as having a quality of "the numinous," referencing the light perceived to be behind and shining through the experience[3]. Abraham Heschel called them moments of "radical amazement.[4]" Martin Buber wrote that what was experienced was a "you" rather than an "it," that they had a relational quality[5]. Maslow, in writing about peak experiences, wrote about them as "seeing the way things *really* are."[6] Mircea Eliade, the great scholar of comparative religions in the mid-20th century, called them experiences of "the golden world,"[7] inferring seeing through the veil of this world into the next. Most all researchers and writers refer to them as direct experiences of the sacred, of the holy, or of God or of the divine spirit. Marcus Borg, who himself had many such experiences, recognized that there are many people, Christian and non-Christian alike, current and past, for whom the divine spirit is *known*, that is, is experienced as real, not a hypothetical being who may or may not exist and whom we can only believe in, but one who is deeply and profoundly known. I love how he put it in a book chapter describing his return to mysticism: "It has . . . shaped my understanding of religions in general and major religious figures, including the central figures of the biblical tradition: Moses, the prophets, Jesus, Paul and

3. Otto, *Idea of the Holy*, 7.

4. Heschel, *Man Is Not Alone*.

5. Buber, *I and Thou*.

6. Maslow, *Religions, Values and Peak Experience*.

7. Eliade, *The Sacred and the Profane*, 20–21.

others. They were all people for whom God, the sacred, the more, was an experiential reality. That is where their way of seeing—their wisdom, their passion, and their courage—came from. They didn't simply believe strongly in God; they *knew* God . . . that God is real and the Bible and Christianity are the Christian story of relationship with God, 'the more,' 'what is.'"[8]

Some stories are striking. One former colleague of mine related many such experiences, with one in particular standing out. Lori was a chaplain, student and close co-worker. She had a soft and open and compassionate way about her; at the same time, she literally emanated what I can only describe as loving energy. I was often struck by her radiance. One day she was walking down the hallway of the unit in the medical center where she was providing spiritual care as a staff chaplain. A mother and her six-year-old child were in one of the rooms, with the door open, the young boy extremely ill with a virulent form of meningitis. The mom saw Lori walking by and waved her down, asking her if she would please come in to pray with her and her son. Of course she would. Lori inquired about what was going on, and the young boy, very attuned to Lori, weakly raised his head and said "Mom, she has white light." "I know son, that's why I asked her to come in," replied mom, asking Lori *to put her hand on his shoulder*. Lori reports that she then offered her prayer, and seemed to lose track of time, as if it had been standing still. When she finished her prayer and opened her eyes, the boy was sitting up, and simply reported, "Mom, I'm okay now." And indeed, amazingly, he was. Lori later learned from the nurse that the boy had not been expected to survive the end of her shift. And she further learned that he was discharged from the hospital that evening. The physician's note simply said, "spontaneous remission."

What are we to make of such things? Could it be that the radiance in her countenance with which I was so familiar was something more than just good nutrition and ample sleep? Could it be that her "white light" was some kind of healing energy that was flowing into her from the divine source in ways that neither she nor I could understand?

Some months later, I received a call from a young woman asking if she could volunteer with our department. She had a love for children and would like to visit them in the pediatrics unit. I liked her voice and energy on the phone, but had to reluctantly tell her that volunteering in our department wouldn't be possible, due to privacy concerns and training and credentialing regulations. Still, I invited her to come to the office so we

8. Borg, *Days of Awe and Wonder*, 43.

could meet, having a sense that she had just entered my life for a purpose. I had the sense that it was important for me to meet with her somehow.

Rachel told me that she was in private practice to help others become spiritually whole and to work through their barriers to fulfillment and contentment. And she, too, had a radiance about her and a certain wisdom and presence that I had always found to be very rare. I inquired further, and she told me that even as a very young child she knew that she was uniquely gifted, different, attuned to things "on another plane." She said it was as if the divine spirit would "download" images and timeless truths and healing energies to her, and that she was often surrounded by and accompanied by "mystical beings" to guide her and support her. I was reminded of Bob Dylan's comment when asked how in the world he was able to write so many incredible songs. "They're just downloaded," he replied. "They're not my songs. I just sit down and put pen to paper, and they are provided to me." I found Rachel fascinating. And lovely. I wanted Lori to meet her, so I paged her, and she arrived just a few minutes later. When she walked into the office, Rachel's eyes immediately filled with tears. "Oh, my goodness," she exclaimed, "your light is the brightest, whitest light I've ever seen. Do you know that you are a healer?" And then Lori's eyes filled with tears as well, as did mine. Again, what do we do with such things?

I asked my friend Bryce about his experiences and perspective; Bryce, like Rachel, is spiritually gifted and "sees" energy fields and white light and is able even to communicate with the "beings" who come into his vision and consciousness routinely. He would often comment on the intensity of the light emanating from me, even when I was less than self-aware. It was difficult for me, at first, to know what to do with his reflections. This seemed to be another whole level beyond my understanding of spiritual experiences. Here was someone relating the ability to actually communicate and channel energy from another plane of existence. Yet, he never offered anything without being asked; he was always humble about it, even shy to discuss it. I brought him in to dialogue with my students on several occasions, and he was always aware of his different-ness, always so respectful of those who didn't have similar experiences. But his wisdom was fascinating, even transcendent, as if he was being provided with some insight or awareness that I couldn't quite access, some hidden knowledge.

On one occasion, he looked at one of my students and asked her about her pain. "What do you mean?" she asked. "You have a lot of pain in your right shoulder" he responded. "How do you know that?" she asked, with incredulity. "The color of the light emanating from your shoulder suggests a deep injury." At this my student, a thirty-eight year old highly educated, professional minister, appeared a bit stunned. She told him and us that it was an old volleyball injury from college, and that she had recently re-injured it and that she was really struggling with the pain, fearing she would need surgery. "Would you like me to see what I could do?" Bryce asked. She would. He stood behind her, closed his eyes, and began to move his fingers back and forth about an inch above her shoulder. He did this for about a minute. Then he sat back down, looked at her and said, "You're about 75 percent better. Try lifting your arm above your head." "I haven't been able to do that since I was eighteen," she said. "You can now," Bryce replied, and she broke down in tears of relief and amazement as she did so.

I was fortunate to work with many licensed clinical social workers over the years, wonderful colleagues all. Scott Janssen is a hospice social worker in North Carolina, who is also a writer. He describes beautifully a representative conversation of what so many of us who worked with dying people so often heard:

> *For months, as I've visited Evan as his hospice social worker, he has been praying to die. In his early 90s, he has been dealing with colorectal cancer for more than four years, and he is flat tired out. As he sees it, the long days of illness have turned his life into a tedious, meaningless dirge with nothing to look forward to other than its end. He's done, finished. He often talks about killing himself.*
>
> *On this visit, though, his depression seems to have lifted. He's engaged and upbeat—and this sudden about-face arouses my suspicions: Has he decided to do it? Is he planning a way out? "You seem to feel differently today than on other visits," I say casually. "What's going on?"*
>
> *He looks at me cryptically. "Do you believe in ghosts?" he asks. It's not the first time a patient has asked me this. People can have unusual experiences when they reach the end of life: near-death or out-of-body experiences, visitations from spiritual beings, messages delivered in dreams, synchronicities or strange behaviors by animals, birds, even insects. "There are all kinds of ghosts," I respond seriously. "What kind are you talking about?" "You remember me telling you about the war?" he asks. How could I forget? He'd traced his long-standing depression to his time as a supply officer for a World War II combat hospital. The war, he'd said, had soured him on the idea that anything good could come from humans and left him feeling unsafe and alone. "I remember."*

141

"There's something I left out," he says. "Something I can't explain." He goes on to describe one horrific, ice-cold autumn day: Casualties were coming in nonstop. He and others scrambled to transport blood-soaked men on stretchers from rail cars to triage, where those with a chance were separated from those who were goners. "I'd been hustling all day. By the time the last train arrived, my back felt broken, and my hands were numb from the cold." He grimaces and swallows hard. "What happened when the last train got there?" I ask softly. "We were hauling one guy, and my grip on the stretcher slipped." Tears roll down his face. "When he hit the ground, his intestines oozed out. Steam rose up from them as he died." Evan rubs his hands as though they were still cold.

"Later that night I was on my cot crying. Couldn't stop crying about that poor guy, and all the others I'd seen die. My cot was creaking, I was shaking so hard. I even started getting scared that I was going insane with the pain." I nod, waiting for him to continue. "Then I looked up," he says. "Saw a guy sitting on the end of my cot. He was wearing a World War I uniform, with one of those funny helmets. He was covered in light, like he was glowing in the dark." "What was he doing?" I ask. Evan starts crying and laughing at the same time. "He was looking at me with love. I could feel it. I'd never felt that kind of love before." "What was it like to feel that kind of love?" "I can't put it in words." He pauses. "I guess I just felt like I was worth something, like all the pain and cruelty wasn't what was real." "What was real?" "Knowing that no matter how screwed-up and cruel the world looks, on some level, somehow, we are all loved. We are all connected."

This turned out to be the first of several paranormal visits. Each time the specter arrived, he'd wordlessly express love and leave Evan with a sense of peace and calm. "After the war, the visits stopped," he says. "Years later, I was cleaning out Mom's stuff after she died, and I found an old photograph. It was the same guy. I looked on the back, and Mom had written the words 'Uncle Calvin, killed during World War I, 1918.'"

We talk some more, then I ask, "What does this have to do with your being in a better mood?" "He's back," he whispers, staring out the window. "Saw him last night on the foot of my bed. He spoke this time." "What'd he say?" "He told me he was here with me. He's going to help me over the hill when it's time to go." As I'm formulating more questions, Evan surprises me by asking one of his own. "You ever have something strange happen? Something that tells you that no matter how bad it looks, you're connected with something bigger, and it's going to be okay?"

A memory flashes into my mind. It was 35 years ago. It was after midnight, and I was asleep in a graduate-student apartment at Syracuse University. A siren's blare woke me, so loud it sounded like it was inside the room. Adrenaline pumping, heart pounding like a hammer, I sat up and wondered what had happened. Was it a dream? From outside, I distinctly heard what sounded like a two-man stretcher crew talking. "Bring it here quick," one guy told the other. I heard a gurney being rolled across asphalt. I went to the window and pulled back the curtain, certain there was trouble outside.

The night was silent. Nothing was stirring in the parking lot. No one was there. Just before daybreak, Dad called to tell me that just a few hours earlier, my uncle Eddie had been killed in an automobile collision. That was a tough day. As night fell once more, questions filled my head: Why did this happen? What was he experiencing when it ended? Was he scared?

On the kitchen table sat a beat-up radio; some kind of malfunction occasionally caused it to turn off or on for no apparent reason. As my questions swirled, the radio turned on, and I heard the opening chords of the Beatles' song "Let It Be." Not being a fan, I'd never listened closely to the song before—but this time, I did. The music and words filled me with an almost otherworldly sense of peace and comfort. The song ended. Shortly after, the radio cut off. For years, I tried to explain away those events. It must have been a dream, I told myself. Or some kind of fabricated "memory" to fool myself into thinking that Uncle Eddie and I were connected in that moment. As for the radio, it was nothing but a random coincidence. Any other conclusion is just wishful thinking. Inside, though, a part of me knew it was real. After nearly 30 years as a hospice social worker, I'm certain of it. And I have patients like Evan to thank: dying patients who have convinced me that the world we inhabit is lovingly mysterious and eager to support us, especially during times of disorientation and crisis. It even sends messages of love and reassurance now and then when we're in pain.

I return to the present. Evan is looking at me, waiting for an answer. I feel grateful that he's pulled up these memories. Outside, a flock of crows takes off in unison from the branches of an ancient oak. "Yeah," I say with a nod. "I guess I have."[9]

Perhaps this is the place to revisit the stories about the "resurrection" of Jesus, so significant is it to the whole expansion of Christianity; and so problematic as well to those outside the tradition. But perhaps it need neither be the litmus test of faith nor the stumbling block of doubt. Bryce and

9. Janssen, *"A Tale of Two Visitors"*.

Rachel have the gift (and burden) of seeing other "beings," the spirits of those who have died, in something resembling human form. It is clear to both of them that we continue on past death into something new. And Anita had a sense as she lay dying of having always existed, of being eternal, of being more than her body, of being pure and loving energy. And countless patients tell stories of seeing and even talking with their loved ones during their near-death experiences. Perhaps it was no different with Jesus and his friends; he "appeared" to them after his death, the gospel writers state, and he assured them of his love for them. In a couple of the stories, they did not recognize him until later, or until he spoke to them. And when he spoke, he spoke lovingly. Is that story any different than the stories and experiences of Bryce and Rachel and Anita and Evan? Perhaps such recognition of such *through the veil* connections and timelessness is reflective of the tenets of quantum physics. Perhaps it is what constitutes the nature of the faith of our forefathers and mothers. Perhaps our future dying experiences, too, will transform us all into eternal beings of pure loving energy. And perhaps, in that sense, we are all divine: Jesus, the disciples, Bryce, Rachel, Scott, Evan, Anita—and you and I.

In becoming more spiritually intelligent and aware, we are invited to wrestle with mysticism and spiritual experience. One key component of that process is to explore our understanding of the mind, or more particularly, of consciousness and *un*consciousness, and to look at what we mean by the term, "the collective unconscious."

Recent studies in neuroscience involving meditation and quantum mechanics and neuropsychology show how deeply intertwined and inseparable are the brain and mind, but how distinct as well. We might say that the mind is reflective of the energy and chemical flow within the brain and tied to its functioning, even as it is somehow *more* than the brain and connected to the minds of others. Most would even say today that the mind is both organic *and* has a quality of transcendence and universality about it, being somehow more than the person, more than the one who is the thinker and feeler, and certainly more than the physical brain itself. We might say that we are both "the knower and the known." What a fascinating way to think about our spirituality, and about higher consciousness. We are both the knower and the known. And if that is true then it begs us to ask the question about the insights and moments of new awareness that seem to come from out of the blue—and sometimes even "seeing" what our eyes cannot see and our brains cannot comprehend. How often do you become aware of something, how often do you "sense" something that you haven't seen or heard? My wife and I often catch each other's thoughts, with one of us verbalizing nearly exactly what the other is thinking. And most all of us can report experiences of extra sensory perception (ESP), where all of a sudden we become aware of something happening somewhere else, as if there is a "warp" in the universe. When my dad died from a descending aortic aneurysm, I knew the exact moment, though he was in surgery and I was at home, confirmed when I spoke with the surgeon at the hospital. It was a powerful moment of absolute "knowing."

So, we are more than just bodies then, we are more than just the stuff of the stars. We are also, in some mystical, mysterious ways, the stuff of the divine as well. We are even learning, in fact, that the interplay between the brain and the mind, as they are progressively infused with ever increasing connectivity through advances in technology and the social media, is speeding up the evolution of our species as both are expanding, with the conclusion that we may very well be in the midst of what the cosmologists would call a quantum leap, as noted above. We are evolving rapidly, as a result of their interplay, into higher levels of being.

For instance, we are learning that the brain functions as a sort of repository of the sum total of human experience and evolution and wisdom; that embedded in every cell of the brain is the imprint of everything that has gone before: all the trauma, all the struggle, all the love and joy and happiness; think Jung's archetypes again. An article by Darold Treffert in Scientific American discusses genetic memories, how we know some things that we in fact never learned or experienced.[10] So just stop and think about what that might say about the unconscious, and how vast it is. Do you ever wonder why dysfunction and pain tend to run in some families for generations? When I was working in a chemical dependency treatment center, the staff psychiatrist used to talk about how families with an alcoholic parent tend to have children who struggle with significant co-dependency and emotional maladaptation; those kids, in turn, tend to have children who become chemically dependent, with the pattern often being repeated down through multiple generations. But it is certainly interruptible, with appropriate intervention and learning.

---

10. Treffert, "Genetic Memory."

I like the sense of the brain serving as an *accessible* repository, even if we don't always know how to get at the deeper material, as available to us for our spiritual growth and development. We are learning that the brain itself is constantly shifting and slowly evolving to accommodate new information, that it is in fact malleable and adaptive, that it is influenced and transformed continuously by, for instance, relational dynamics and the moods and thoughts and expressions of others, and by new stimuli that give rise to new insights. The brain functions as a vast neural network, with billions of possible connections, always alight with energy, always synthesizing whatever new comes in through our senses in new ways. Think of how a threatening visual perception will generate an instantaneous response deep in the brain (in the hippocampus and amygdala) producing chemicals and amino acids that get released to generate emotion, and then the subsequent thought and response to fight or flee.

And we are learning new information about how thoughts are formed and what prompts them, and about how energy moves thoughts forward along established neural pathways, but then how new neural pathways get created when we challenge our old perceptions and behavioral patterns, which becomes the process that gives rise to new ways of being. And we are learning how those thoughts are really units of energy that begin to create new realities and new events that, on a quantum level, generate the processes that somehow begin to become the expressions of our desires, with those new realities stimulating new thoughts in an ever expanding circle of creativity and visioning.

Jung wrote about the concept of *synchronicity*[11]. And the internet and contemporary spiritual writing is filled with discussions about what is referred to as the *law of attraction* and the process of *manifestation*. It's fascinating and engaging stuff. Yet to be spiritually intelligent suggests that while it is stimulating to explore and reflect on how things actually work at a quantum level, it is important to note that there is no scientific consensus on how such mechanical processes influence spiritual experience. In truth, most of our reflections on quantum mysticism are considered pseudo-science by physicists and researchers, and rightly so, since as yet we are unable to prove the connections. Yet there is clearly something to it. We know, for instance, that energy becomes mass and mass becomes energy, and we know that light has both the quality of particles (photons) and waves, and we know that we humans—and all things for that matter—are alive with

---

11. Jung, *Synchronicity*, 417–519.

energy, are indeed pure energy at the quantum level, but we don't fully understand the ramifications for how those scientifically-based truths actually play out in the interplay of our collective unconscious or of our relationships with one another or of our hopes and dreams. We can't yet draw firm conclusions, and this is important, because once we settle on a perceived understanding of how things actually work, we are at risk of actually *losing* awareness, of becoming caught in certainty once again, which blinds us to other possibilities.

All that said, we do get inklings. We have experiences of seeing anew, of enlightenment; we undergo transformative changes, we stumble into all sorts of coincidental but wonderfully life-enhancing things, we have experiences of ESP, and our actions tend to follow our thoughts, for better and worse. And so often, we end up, surprisingly, manifesting our desires. In the late 80s I chaired a program committee for my organization and ended up co-hosting a couple of conferences in New Mexico. I loved being there, and thought often, both then and later, about how wonderful it would be to live there someday. At the time, it wasn't even a remote possibility. And yet, here I am today, in a lovely home, fully retired and healthy, and loving being just south of Albuquerque. We are mystical beings; we are more than our bodies. We are connected, unconsciously. We even seem to somehow—mysteriously—influence our own future realities. And we do not fully understand.

Jung described synchronicity as "meaningful coincidence," and he had a clear sense that when something happens "synchronistically," it comes to us as an experience of grace, something that seems intended to enhance our life experience.[12] We get the sense that when something or someone comes into our lives unexpectedly, it feels somehow, intentional or purposeful. I had been single for some years and was sitting in a restaurant on a Friday evening, mindlessly perusing a local newspaper. When I came to the personal ads in the back (this was pre-internet days) my eyes fell on one ad and it captured my attention. There were all sorts of questions I might have asked myself, looking back—why that ad, why then, what happened for it to capture my attention—but instead I just then and there decided to respond to it, and I have been happily married to Gail ever since. There were times early in our relationship where we were acutely aware of the synchronicity of the moment, recognizing how we enhanced each other's lives, how easily we connected as if we both had the same hopes and dreams, how meeting

12. Jung, *Synchronicity*, 417–519.

each other had a quality of destiny about it. Were we just "lucky" or was something else at play? Did our mutual but unconscious desires somehow shape what played out? Did the energy generated by Gail's intentionality somehow pull in my awareness and provide me with an opportunity (think process theology) to assent to that which would make my life full of love and happiness?

The "law" of attraction and the concept of manifestation, as described in popular literature, suggest that our state of consciousness and attitude play a role in bringing about our reality, that the energy we put out comes back to us, corresponding to our inner state. If we have not integrated the pain of our lives, and end up having thoughts colored by resentment, anger, bitterness etc., then those thoughts seem to "attract" a similar energy. Our external reality becomes colored by our internal reality. Conversely, when we live forward from a place of healing and contentment and gratitude, we might say that a similar energy comes to us, is "attracted" to us, and our positive hopes and desires somehow are made manifest. On the one hand, we can all relate to that simple concept; people who commit to being content and happy and kind tend to have people in their lives with similar orientations. People who are emotionally negative and harsh, tend to spin down into problematic relationships and workaday struggles. We all get that. But on the other hand, such a dynamic flow of energy at the quantum level probably can't be put in a box or turned into some sort of formula for abundant living. It may very well be that we play a role in shaping our reality, but when we get caught up in attempting to manifest our hidden ego needs and self-centered desires, we tend to become frustrated and disappointed, and we get pulled away from the wonder of the creative energy.

I have wrestled with the trendy writings and films such as "The Secret" and "What the Bleep Do We Know" that seem to suggest we can actually bring abundance into our lives through disciplined manifesting of desired outcomes. Spiritual intelligence seems, instead, to always point us toward humility and to embracing the divine mysteries with trust, hope and anticipation of the wonder of the unfolding. When our consciousness and spiritual intelligence is raised, we recognize that it is never just about the self, that it is always about honoring our innate sense of belonging as fully-fledged members of the human tribe, passionately concerned about the future of the planet and about the well-being of one another. As we do that, we get in touch with "awe" once again, like that first time I really saw the universe laid out against the night skies. Some writers have even begun referring to the psychology of raised consciousness and communal awareness as the "science of awe." A recent article in Psychology Today explains the phenomenon as "a sense of embeddedness into collective folds and an increase in pro-social behaviors such as kindness, self-sacrifice, cooperation and resource-sharing. Experiences that arouse awe can help us to re-conceptualize our sense of self, our role in society and, from a more cosmic perspective, our place in the universe."[13]

The incredible explosion of scientific knowledge that is occurring in quantum and astrophysics—no longer just theory, but real knowledge—is reshaping the whole conversation for us seeking greater spiritual intelligence. Today that means talking about the blending of theology and cosmology and evolution into a new level of awareness and higher consciousness in what is rapidly becoming a post-religious world. The challenge is to cultivate a deepened soul even as we embrace these new realities, and then empower others to move toward that higher level of consciousness as well, to acceptance of changing circumstances, and to greater peace of mind.

I am drawn to that because I have been humbled by my experiences, both personal and professional, and because I have learned over the years that literally everyone is hungry to be known, hungry to understand, hungry to be nurtured and cared about, hungry to be touched. Hungry to adapt to a changing world. Hungry for meaning and acceptance and transformation. Hungry to be loved. Hungry to have their souls fed in new ways. Everyone. Every human person; its intrinsic to our species. A wise psychiatrist in my early training told me once that everyone needs two things in life in order to thrive, and those two things are nurture and belonging. And we are all hungry for them; there just never seems to be enough to go around.

So, if you are a chaplain or a therapist or a helper—or just someone wanting to deepen your own understanding—it seems our primary task is to *nurture* each other, to enter into relationship, to allow ourselves to love, if you will, to create connections that begin to tap into the hunger to be nurtured and to belong. We've got to work with ourselves and each other to figure out how to do that *meaningfully*. Talk about boundaries all you want, if we're not loving our patients and clients, if we are not caring for them *deeply*, then we're not providing the essential element of spiritual care. The same is true for our students, for those of you who are teachers, and for our children, for those of you who are parents. The task isn't just to facilitate learning, it is to facilitate awareness and growth and to help

13. Stone, "The Emerging Science of Awe."

them thrive. So—nurturing and belonging, the two key building blocks of spiritual health and wholeness for everyone.

And why are they so important? Because if spiritual intelligence and spiritual care are becoming more and more about spiritual transformation, and the physical re-alignment of energy, and adaptation to changing circumstances, and congruence and healing, than it is, say, about religious belief systems and dogma—and it is—then we need to *open up* the space between us and each other so that healing can happen most fully. And we do well to open it up not as empty space but as inviting, compassionate space which hurting and hungry people will want to enter; indeed, into which they will feel compelled to enter. Love and nurture are *evocative*, they draw people forward into self-disclosure, into reflective relationship, into the intimate encounter. The space we open up becomes the place where *the unconscious* can be given expression that might not otherwise be given.

Whether that is done through generating the expression of suppressed feelings, or through guided meditation, or through nurturing touch, or through sacred writings or images that tap into the sacred center in each of us, such expression becomes the pathway and the process for healing and personal growth. We're talking about providing *presence* here, not presence as in being a good listener or a nice person, but presence as in dynamic engagement, as in generating deep and transformative connections, as in the creation of truly sacred, creative space. And what is it, actually, that comes forward into that healing space? There is good reason to think that what comes forward are the images, thoughts, memories and repressed emotions of all previous experiences, together with the conclusions we drew about them at the time—what most of us tend to be referring to when we talk about the unconscious. What tends to come forward are the repressed feelings and associated unconscious memories and experiences that need to be healed.

I have been fascinated by the rise in conspiracy theories and delusional thinking these last couple years in the United States. I have wondered about what a person is seeking—or lacking—when embracing "group think" that has no actual basis in reality. The zenith of this has been the QAnon phenomena, with disinformation rapidly spread via the internet, and bizarre conclusions (about Democrats manipulating the Presidential election, about Covid vaccines being a vehicle of mind control, etc.) being seen as key motivations for taking up arms and threatening the political process. Families have separated, friendships have been broken, political alliances have been shattered. Even more bizarrely, some nationally-elected officials support and proliferate what has come to be called The Big Lie, and get caught up in trying to preserve their own supposed-power through deceit and manipulation and the refusal to speak the truth. And this all culminated in the assault on the US Capitol.

The lack of emotional awareness, the abject refusal to engage with reason, the psychological blindness, the spiritual emptiness, all of it leaves us shaken and anxious. Can we possibility find a way forward and begin to explore processes of mutual self-disclosure with people who are caught up in such constricted thinking? Can we find a way to practice true presence, to create the space for spiritual reflection? Johns Hopkins University clinical psychologist William Richards believes that, in addition to pain and trauma, ethics and morality are hard-wired into the brain, that they are perhaps "genetically encoded" within the human organism.[14] If so, there is reason to be optimistic and to work to find ways to where such natural impulses can be coaxed into healing expression. Yet without some heightened spiritual awareness to hold the human race together, we can see that we are at risk of devolving into fractious and warring tribes once again, where life becomes threatened. Alienation is rampant. Depression and suicide are increasing, as are acts of violence. Deaths from opioid abuse increased by 38% between 2019 and 2020[15], and it has been a crisis for several years. As the environmental crisis has deepened, as the income gap has grown and as poverty has spread, as egregious racism has been brought out into the open, as religion has largely failed to bring any cohesion, as autocratic leaders have gained power around the world—we find ourselves at something of a crossroads. Can we find a way forward once again? Can we rediscover the science of awe? Can we possibly link into the collective unconscious in ways we haven't yet discovered to begin the healing and stimulate cooperation and collaboration?

The thing is that our ancestors, in order to survive, paid an inordinate amount of attention to threatening or negative experiences. They became extremely skilled at surviving through threatening circumstances. But the downside is that as a result, *reaction to threat* is by far the more prominent metabolic response for us today. We are, simply stated, reactive individuals,

---

14. Richards, *Sacred Knowledge.*

15. Centers for Disease Control and Prevention, *"Overdose Deaths Accelerating During COVID-19."*

with our reactivity much more developed than our desire to approach the positive.

So, think about all the ramifications of that, both in ourselves and in our patients or students or relationships. Even as ethics and morality may be hard-wired into our brains, so are we evolutionarily *inclined* toward caution, self-protection, and aggression. When we create space for people to come forward into transparent self-expression in spiritual care—people who are under stress or facing threatening life changes or, say, a terminal diagnosis—the most likely expression out of their unconscious repositories will be expressions of anxiety or distrust, along with reactivity to threat and loss of control. As a matter of fact, when we do that job well—creating a safe harbor and sense of acceptance and unconditional positive regard—we will make space for and receive those difficult, unresolved things from our patients, and facilitate their integration. That is a very good thing, because that is how the process of healing begins, allowing people to access their pre-frontal cortexes (where we can apply rational thinking and do problem solving) and begin to process *reasonably* those distressful and unresolved feelings. And here's the challenge: if we become reactive to the expressions of others, or if we haven't settled our own emotional stuff and feel at stake of being rejected, then the space between us becomes less inviting and the opportunity for the other to disclose that which is in their unconscious gets blunted. Ed Friedman's great guidance was that the most important task of maturity is to "lower our own reactivity to the reactivity of others," and that is certainly not an easy thing to do.

So, I prefer to think about the work of spiritual intelligence as *shining light into the darkness*—shining a light into the darkness of unresolved pain and unconscious struggle and maladaptation, shining light into our own and each other's lack of awareness if you will. The metaphor of light and darkness is apt and powerful, because your brain tends to grab onto and hold negative experiences (as a means of learning how to survive) and it tends to let the positive ones slip away, which explains why we have to learn some lessons over and over again. And it explains why we never seem to get enough affirmation. It just slides on through. And the hippocampus buries the negative words and experiences pretty deep in our psyches. Deep in our *unconscious*, if you will. And it can have pretty profound effects. Most of the maladaptive behaviors and illnesses described in the DSM-5 are the result of pathological thought processes creating chemical changes in the brain, most all of which result from the subtle yet powerful effects of abuse, abandonment and diminishment (insults to the psyche and the soul) in childhood. Or think of post-traumatic stress and the reactions of soldiers and others to the horrors of war. We all have friends who've served in Viet Nam or Iraq or Afghanistan who continue to manifest the pain of their experiences and who seem plagued by anxiety or agitation or distress, chemical processes resulting from their initial perceptions of traumatizing events.

And it happens in health care as well. I had a COPD patient once who had been very ill, and at the crisis point she had been essentially sedated and chemically paralyzed to allow the lungs total rest. But apparently, she had not been provided appropriate pain medication, since her pain couldn't be accurately assessed due to the sedation. The trauma of being paralyzed and in pain, however, was certainly recorded and stored by her brain, even though she was sedated, because on her next visit to the hospital she became extremely anxious without understanding why. When we found an article that identified how patients under the paralyzing drug *pavulon* tend not to get adequate pain medication, it validated her experience and helped her to understand her unconscious responses to what her psyche had experienced as traumatic. And we ended up changing the ICU protocol as a result. Bringing those negative experiences out from the darkness of being deeply *repressed into* the hippocampus, *up into* the light—and the phrase "the light of God" certainly fits here—where they can be integrated and transformed, significantly contributes to the definition of our work.

You get the sense that I am really most interested in who we are, how we got here, what's really going on within us and around us, and where we are headed. Great philosophical and existential questions all. Perhaps becoming spiritually intelligent means, above all, that we become fully conscious of what's really going on, mindful of deepening our souls as we do, and attuned to facilitating resilience and greater spiritual vitality in each other. To reference the core of the Judeo-Christian tradition once again, we might harken back to what Jesus did to raise the consciousness of his friends and followers and to shine light into darkness: he appealed to the whole person, to the heart, the body, the senses, and the imagination, as well as to the mind, calling them to attune themselves to the divine mysteries, to pause and reflect, to discern the movement of the spirit, to listen deeply and to look through the veil, to trust their perceptions, to have those "with eyes, see," and to have those "with ears, hear . . . ." We can't afford to claim that our ways of seeing and acting are strictly a private matter any longer. When we give into anger or helplessness or despair, we somehow seem to add to their power and our own potential gets diminished. Conversely, when we see the possibilities for healing and transformation, in ourselves and others, our creativity awakens and we become that light once again, opening the force field that directs itself toward the transformation of all.

Chapter Twelve

Integration

A parable:

A man had three children, and taught them a spiritual practice:
the act of walking with him each morning to the mountain,
picking up one pebble, carrying it to the far side of the stream, and
setting it down again.

On these walks, the man and his children noticed many things:
the beauty of the sunrise, the grandeur of the open sky, the impor-
tance of being together in quiet respect.

This gentle practice became so meaningful to his three children,
that they taught it to their children: walking to the same mountain,
picking up a single pebble, and delivering it to the same place across
the river.

And thus, it continued with the children's children, when they
had grown,
and with their children, and on down, through the generations.
Until it became so, that the mountain was moved.

—UNKNOWN

THE CONCEPT OF *INTEGRATION* references having our thoughts and words and actions reflect our most deeply held values, beliefs and self-understanding. It means being able to use past painful experiences constructively to inform proactive ways of being. It means being able to keep perspective and remain self-differentiated when interactions become challenging. It means being experienced by others as congruent and as having deep integrity. It means living authentically and transparently. It means being clear about what motivates us, touches us, inspires us, and guides us. And it means being emotionally and spiritually intelligent enough to live consciously and intentionally.

Emotionally-evolved and healthy people tend to do that naturally, and their words and their actions generally line up with their intent. But those of us who live with painful experiences out of our childhoods, or with trauma, or with abuse, or with large and unexplored "shadows," tend to struggle with congruence. We become prone to reactive and dysfunctional behaviors, often responding out of a sense of victimization. We develop and wall off private thoughts, we struggle with identity and develop a sense of connectedness only with like-minded people, becoming tribal and rigid. We struggle with self-esteem and self-love, and so seek affirmation externally. And the reality is that most all of that is done unconsciously. Unless we do our own internal work and settle the hurts and resentments and frustrations, unless we have guides and mentors and clear boundaries as we develop, we are at risk of acting out, of over-expressing, of being seen as intense or aloof or as not to be trusted. We remain unintegrated. We only begin to integrate more fully as we become more emotionally mature and spiritually astute.

The concept of *emotional intelligence* that has been prominent in the self-help literature for the last couple of decades is a key factor. Dan Goleman and others have identified five essential elements: self-awareness, motivation, self-regulation, empathy, and adeptness in relationships.[1] A brief word about each:

- *Self-awareness* refers to being able to identify and name what we are feeling and experiencing, first to ourselves and then to others. Crucial to this capability is the ability to stay differentiated in conversation, that is, to name what is being experienced without blame or hurtful projection. For example, *I feel sad when you . . .* , or *I'm aware of wanting to protect myself when you . . . .* It also means we have developed the ability to accurately self-assess, to recognize and acknowledge that which we do not yet know, while remaining humble about that which we do, avoiding the seduction of power or control or the need for recognition. People with this level of emotional intelligence tend to value intrinsic self-affirmation well above extrinsic affirmation.

---

1. Golman, *Working with Emotional Intelligence.*

- *Motivation* refers to developing the internal drive to develop effective ways to express core values and generally just do things better. Rather than the popular sense of being driven to achieve one's goals, emotionally intelligent people develop the inherent sense of wanting to do better and be more; as a matter of fact, they will come to value self-sacrifice as a way to help *everyone* do better, finding a sense of purpose in the larger mission. Intrinsically motivated people tend to be optimistic, encouraging and empowering, visionary and grateful.

- *Self-regulation* means to develop the capacity to manage both impulsive and compulsive urges and distressing emotions. People who effectively self-regulate find ways to stay composed, to seek out solutions rather than fall back into arguments or rationalizations or excuses, and they hold themselves (and others) accountable to high, yet reasonable, standards. They trust and are trustworthy. We learn to embrace our shadows and transform them, we learn to be gentle with ourselves and to let go of internal demand and expectation, we learn to embrace uncertainty and hold everything lightly.

- *Empathy* is that quality that is so essential to effective spiritual care. It refers to being able to be and stay emotionally *present*, valuing the perspectives and emotions of others without judgment, without distraction. People with this competency take a service orientation naturally, seeking the best for others, helping them grow according to each other's desires. They tend to appreciate and promote diversity and political awareness, shaping social networks toward communally-held values.

- *Adeptness in relationships* reflects the capacity to remain flexible while being clear and direct, to be self-defining while remaining empathic towards others' self-definitions and self-awareness, and to honor boundaries while remaining influential. It is the key practical skill of seeking to become more emotionally intelligent. People who are adept in relationships tend to be well-liked, at ease socially, and taken seriously by others.

In my life-coaching practice, the dominant concern of my clients has been learning how to strengthen and deepen their relationships, and the focus is almost always on their primary relationship with their spouse or partner. It is certainly where so many of us live and breathe. And people recognize inherently that if they can learn and grow around how to be an effective and successful marriage partner, that skill will generalize to other social and professional relationships. They recognize that the first step is their own integration, which makes space for mutual exploration and joint learning. A typical story tends to be about slowly recognizing the inability to empathize, to self-regulate and to recognize and honor boundaries. Once that lack is acknowledged, growth begins to happen and both partners may choose to begin to learn together. Developing emotional intelligence becomes the key that unlocks successful marriages. With national divorce statistics hovering just over 50%, it seems too many of us fail to choose the pathway of vulnerability and empathy.

Mine was the typical story. My first marriage, in my early twenties, was seemingly doomed from the beginning. Neither of us was emotionally evolved, with both of us looking to the other to complete ourselves, rather than each doing our own internal work. I was a rather shallow extrovert, my wife the stoic introvert. As a result, we both tended to withdraw into self-defensive postures and expressions of recrimination. We were caught in a continuing cycle of fighting, withdrawing, resenting, making up, and fighting again. Typically, such situations eventually break, leading either to surrender and a desire to get help and learn, or to a separation and divorce. Because the stakes felt so high to me, we went through years of the first, only to have the deep pain of a late-term miscarriage—and the failure to find a way to healing that profound sense of loss—lead to the final break.

I look back on that experience now with humility and kindness toward those two young and emotionally un-self-aware and unresourceful people. And so began my exploration and desire to learn, to become more emotionally intelligent, to become more spiritually aware and aligned.

❀ ❀ ❀ ❀ ❀

Emotional intelligence and spiritual intelligence reflect each other, and when integrated, hold out the promise of fullness of life. Complementing the essential elements of emotional intelligence, we might summarize the essential elements of spiritual intelligence as these: sacralization of life and the world, inviting communion, accepting reality, living in the present, and trusting the process of becoming. Again, a word about each.

- *Sacralization of life and the world as a manifestation of the divine spirit.* We start with recognizing that all things are sacred, that all of life—and all the creatures and features within life—are an expression and creation of the divine energies pervading the universe. From the quantum building blocks to the grandest stars, all is borne from the sacred mysteries. This means we treat everything with deep respect, with compassion when hurting, with love for one another as the norm. We seek to enhance beauty, to celebrate learning, to live into joy and gratitude. All things are from the divine source, and the divine source is for all things and in all things, and we find meaning in the unfolding.

- *Inviting communion* references opening ourselves to divine inspiration (being *in*-spired, taking in the divine spirit) and to divine guidance. Becoming spiritually intelligent means listening *for* that guidance and living *into* the expectation that we are being actively loved into our process of growth and insight and understanding. When thoughts and ideas and feelings come into us, we have placed before us the choice of assenting to co-creation, or of turning away, in a never-ending process of making things new. When we pray and meditate, we align with the spirit's desires for our lives, and gain a deepened recognition of the spirit's engagement with us, of the call to heightened consciousness and to the expansion of our being.

- *Accepting reality.* We learn to accept ourselves, one another, and all things as they are, for what they are. Acceptance allows introspection, movement forward, and personal growth. When we accept reality, our spirit is at ease and we stay in our sacred center, we become able to be generative, able to create, and able to love. Accepting one another as the reflection of the divine and of ourselves allows for understanding, community and freedom. Resisting reality generates emotions of lowered frequency and our energy and light dim. Like attracts like; when we give off negative vibes or dark energy, it attracts dark energy in return, and we become at greater risk of pain. When we give off positive energy and brighter light, positive energy is attracted, and we thrive.

- *Living in the present* suggests the wisdom of being mindful and present to what is happening within and in front of us in the present moment. When we do, we are not plagued by painful memories or resentments or hurts; when we do, we do not feel anxious about what has or hasn't happened yet, and we do not feel afraid. It says repeatedly, in both the Hebrew and Christian scriptures, "Do not be afraid." It is usually spoken with the implication that to become afraid is to fail to live in the present and it is to give in to the darker frequencies. When we stay in the present moment, we can be mindful, attuned, aware, present and loving. And we will be neither resentful nor afraid.

- *Trusting the process of becoming* suggests that the great measure of our spirituality isn't faith per se, but trust. We trust that we are in the process of becoming more than we were before, that we can learn and grow and find still greater happiness and satisfaction and joy and love. We trust that we will be cared for whatever comes. We trust that things are unfolding toward yet still fuller expressions of love and beauty and creativity and wonder. We trust that our spirit is eternal, that it pre-existed us and will continue to exist beyond death. We trust that as we tap into the collective unconscious, we will be sustained by the sacred source.

Mountains are moved when we, first, get it together internally, doing our work and integrating our learning, and then secondly, when we enter into community with one another, as nurturing progenitors, bringing others along and sharing in mutual hopes and dreams. It wasn't until the last few years of my career that I thought I was doing my best work, as I slowly learned to set aside my own ego in favor of being mindful to nurture others. And where there is nurture and belonging, there is learning and thriving.

The integration of emotional and spiritual intelligence with our lived experiences makes for living authentically, deeply, compassionately, and hopefully. As we embrace the great story of our evolution and development, as we come to trust the engagement of the divine not only with the human community but with each of us as individuals, and as we move toward intimate expressions of vulnerability and love in our relationships, we become gentled into an experience of peace, and all things become well.

Could this then be the pathway both for living a deeply meaningful and rewarding life, and for overcoming that which divides us? You can see how the issue of differing religious beliefs remains problematic in our society and throughout the whole human community. To hold tightly to religious beliefs that may not be grounded in reality is to distinguish ourselves in ways that split us off from that community. Rigidly held beliefs keep us separated rigidly. With the rapid evolution of human travel and migration, such reactivity has become a challenging concern, leading to all sorts of reactivity and discrimination. I used to say to my students that it didn't matter what they believed, and that it was none of my business. What did matter, and which was my business, was how they treated people and the world and how they found personal peace and happiness. My business was and is about moving toward greater emotional and spiritual integration. Today in America, we have large numbers of conservative evangelical Christians as well as moderate and progressive Christians; we have Orthodox, Conservative, Reform, and ethnic Jews; we have Shia Muslims and Sunni Muslims and other lesser known iterations; we have Taoists and Confucianists and Shintoists; we have Mormons and Adventists and Jehovah's Witnesses; we have those who practice native religious expressions and those who follow their own unique inclinations. Can we be a society that embraces all as legitimate and sacred? We can, but likely only if we move toward greater and deeper personal integration, toward focusing on spiritual intelligence rather than religious beliefs.

Chapter Thirteen

How, then, shall we live?

"The work goes on, the cause endures, the hope still lives, and the dreams shall never die."

—EDWARD KENNEDY, *CONCESSION SPEECH,* 1980

"Life isn't about finding yourself. Life is about creating yourself."

—GEORGE BERNARD SHAW, *AN UNSOCIAL SOCIALIST*

WE ARE AMAZINGLY COMPLEX and magnificently gifted creatures. We are the embodiment of the divine creative spirit that energizes life; we are the universe becoming conscious of itself; we are made of star stuff and we shine every bit as brightly and beautifully. We are the manifestation of divine love.

Getting in touch with awe and amazement and gratitude is the first step in developing spiritual intelligence, since it both recognizes our profound beauty and potential and brings us to the point of self-emptying humility. In such a place, we open ourselves to "the mysteries" as grateful receivers and curious responders. We begin to seek the "more," the ineffable, the profound. And we begin to make meaning, living in the present moment, trusting the unfolding. We become less concerned with ourselves and more concerned with one another, more wanting to love, more seeking to build up; more wanting to be in partnership with the creative processes, more willing to assent to the cues and pulls and prompts that come to us.

So, seeking to become more spiritually aware and attuned is to do more than just feed our own souls. The process of spiritual reflection isn't intended as an ego-driven exercise to increase our own happiness, though that may certainly be a result. Rather, it is to equip us to live outwardly and forward-leaning, to get us outside of our internal self-recriminations, and to begin to express our core spiritual identities as lovers and givers and healers and creators. It is to make sense of life and fill us with belonging. Religions evolved over the course of human history to help us make meaning and to generate a sense of place and community that would feed us with that experience of connection and relationship. It was never about *beliefs*. Religious expressions weren't established to have us focus on the nature of the divine per se, they were all about honoring our feelings of awe and amazement and gratitude and hope and our natural desire to care for and about one another—until they were corrupted and distorted. What good does it do us to reflect only on ourselves? Too often, we get caught up in our shortcomings and in our lack of understanding.

Instead, we move toward greater spiritual intelligence as we set about *clearing* our minds—getting out of our own way, so to speak—to receive the grace and love and guidance being proffered. It is about tuning in to the unfathomable mysteries, and opening ourselves to healing and fulfillment. It is about being more mind*ful*, more aware, more interested and attuned, and it is about quieting the internal noise. The practice of meditation can be extremely helpful in this process, since at its best it allows the mind to open and the self to fall momentarily away. And yet, meditation is just one of the pieces. If we don't want the noise and difficult internal dialogues to come back, we do well to engage a process for healing.

We recognize that the process of opening up and coming to new realizations, of integrating the learning that moves beyond previous assumptions and conclusions, generally gets prompted by a painful experience or by a prolonged sense of dissatisfaction or unhappiness. For most of us, as it was for so many of my patients and students, it is borne out of a health crisis or a loss or an unanticipated change or, as was often the case, out of the forced recognition that to succeed in work and life means to come to grips with who we are. Indeed, I've had my share of such moments, as have most of us.

But the truth is, it doesn't have to be that way. We can raise our awareness and become more mindful—and, as a result, happier and more contented—through the spiritual processes of reading, reflecting on experience, integrating new learning and adapting to unfolding circumstances differently. We can be our own guides here, and we can learn how to support our own fulfillment and flourish in life intentionally and purposefully without all the pain, if we choose to. Some core concepts have been identified that can at least point us toward such a pathway.

The first is that it is generally helpful to know your own narrative, how you became who you've become, including the dynamics and failings of your family. We have to do our internal work. We do well to pay attention to the crisis points in our families' histories, to what was said and what wasn't said, to how painful experiences were processed or repressed, and to the choices we made and to the consequences of those choices. Try to "own" your life, but remember to always be gracious toward yourself. You were shaped by the values, norms and expressions of your parents in powerful ways. Work to understand them and forgive them, both absolutely crucial to transforming internalized shame.

Embracing your own narrative is no small thing. For instance, learning to understand your family context is crucial, and getting an objective sense of how communication happened or not is a key. And not just communication, but also how boundaries were honored or violated, how your autonomy was supported or diminished, how your sense of self (your feelings, your self-understanding) was loved and nurtured or, conversely, how it was shamed by those around you. And as you do so, work to remain objective about it; see it for what it was, without judgment. One of the paradoxes of therapy is that going back into old feelings and experiences runs the risk of re-victimizing ourselves and may cause us to lose objectivity. It is generally not helpful to over-focus on past painful experiences or on unresolved conflicts or hurt feelings, thus the movement away from a psychoanalytic approach in therapy to the current emphasis on resilience and positive psychology. It isn't healing to go back over painful ground with unfettered emotion, though the cathartic experience can certainly open the doors for change if the motivation and desire to do so is there. Instead, change begins to happen best when we seek to understand, when we maintain objective curiosity, when we succeed at honoring where we are currently. We are survivors, and we become thrivers when we do our internal work.

Secondly, it becomes important to practice acceptance and to move intentionally into the present, where there is no pain, only possibility and potential. Can we truly learn to embrace the present moment, where our minds are free of old resentments and attachments? To do so allows us to orient toward the future, toward realizing those possibilities and potential and living into our fullness. As a matter of fact, visualizing our desires and committing to becoming generative—*paying it forward* to use a current catch phrase—and then expressing our energy toward the best interests of others rather than toward our own ego needs, allows for spiritual abundance and peace of mind. Just watch what happens, as the fullness of life unfolds. We can indeed influence the unfolding. As we free ourselves up from all the painful experiences that weigh us down—the three aspects of freedom and enlightened living being nonresistance, nonjudgement, and nonattachment—then we are co-creating happiness and empowerment.

We do well, too, to learn as much as we can about our inherited evolutionary impulses. We come by our stuff naturally; our emotional responses and reactions reflect the human condition. Our so-called shadow side only becomes toxic when we keep it suppressed. Bringing it into awareness gives us choice and freedom. When we stop fighting our demons and orient toward who we are becoming, we become who we want to be. The old adage really applies here: *whatever you fight you strengthen; whatever you resist, persists.* Transformation happens to us when we move away from our own internal struggles and into compassion for the struggles of those around us. And acceptance *is* the key to transformation. I might even say that the more accepting and attuned we become and the more we let go of internal shame and driven-ness, the more energy increases and the more our futures open up. It's very paradoxical, with the paradox itself becoming holy and sacred and serving as the window into deepened understanding and higher consciousness. I like to think that as we "clear the space" the divine spirit enters in and fills us up.

A key part of that process is recognizing the difference between emotions and feelings. I have found it helpful to think about emotions as chemically-driven bodily responses to thoughts I have about my perceptions. Changing my thoughts changes my emotional state. For example, if I bought in, unconsciously, to a family message that people different from me are somehow a threat to my security, then I will generally experience reactive emotions like fear or anxiety when I am around people different from me, which will in turn trigger fight or flight responses or simply get projected out as anger or judgment or condemnation. Think racism or patriarchy. The same is true for anger. I remember trying to teach other educators in my field that if they got angry with a student (or doctor or nurse or, God forbid, a patient) it was a reflection on their own lack of integration and of their inability to stay differentiated. But changing how I *think* about others—becoming curious about why a particular person is acting out, or recognizing that a person different from me might have something to teach me rather than be a threat—will move me into a less toxic emotion and might even provide an opportunity for connection and growth. You can see here that we can't be spiritually healthy until we have integrated our learning and challenged our previous thoughts and transformed our ways of thinking about others.

Feelings, on the other hand, seem to come into us from elsewhere. I tend to think that they are provided to us by the divine source, to bring us into full awareness and depth of engagement. Empathy is a good example. Years ago, I would shy away from people in pain. Today I can't help but feel deeply in the face of human sorrow or tragedy or crisis and I am drawn in. My eyes tend to well up with tears just watching a heart-warming story or an evocative ad on TV for goodness' sake! The feelings flood in. And I find that I am so grateful to be attuned to the suffering and joys of others in such ways; it has so enriched my life. When I am open and attuned, the energy comes into me. I get a sense of being guided toward fullness somehow. When I feel inspired, I am aware that I am being in-spirited. I am being pointed toward something. I am being offered an opportunity to explore a new way of being. So we do well to work mindfully to discern our feelings, and follow their guidance.

All that said, here are four summary steps toward a fuller, more meaningful life and deepened spiritual intelligence:

- *Develop your observer mind.* Get outside of yourself to where you can feel less attached, and therefore less reactive to difficult experiences. Simply put, you are more than your ego. You are more than the voice in your head, more than the one who is the thinker, or the inner critic, or the struggler, or the complainer, or the helper. *You* are the one who *hears* the voices in your head, who *acknowledges* your thoughts and your ego and the contents of your mind from a perspective *outside* your too-often unconscious mind. You are a soul, you are more than your brain, and you can step outside of yourself to regain perspective. You're all familiar with dissociative reactions; this is a similar process, but arising from an integrated source of higher consciousness. I would even say that you are the awareness in the background, the one who is conscious of your consciousness, if you will. It is your divine nature, and it makes all the difference in the world. And for our purposes here, I will just suggest that being caught in your ego represents lower consciousness, while being in your observer mind represents higher consciousness and your capacity to maintain peace and serenity.

- *Embrace your power to heal.* If we are somehow connected into the "Source of all Consciousness" and somehow connected up with everyone and everything else in the universe, then perhaps we really can be the one through whom that sacred and creative energy flows. If indeed we are the manifestation of the divine, then our expressions convey divine intent and our energies will be experienced as healing and sacred. More and more we are embracing this fullness of potential in modalities like Reiki and healing touch and even in massage and yoga. I had a wonderful experience with what was called the Urban Zen program in Los Angeles a few years ago. That was the name of the Integrative Medicine program at UCLA Health. I had two practitioners do what they called a *body scan* of me, asking about any physical or emotional pain that I might be carrying, and then they worked with me to meditate, relax, and stretch, with both of them always maintaining one hand somewhere on my body, never lifting it away. And, as I slowly gave myself over to them and let myself sort of fall into their care if you will, I was mindful of the warmth of their hands, and of the loving energy that flowed from them to me, and of how good I felt when it was over, both physically and emotionally. Amazing. The power to heal. Own it and draw from it to settle your body and to allow it to do its own natural restorative work. And do the same for others; speak a work of compassion, provide an act of love, touch and embrace and support, be kind.

- *Rethink your theology and spiritual beliefs.* What do you really mean when you use the term "God?" What is God really, and what is God really doing? And what do we do about what God is really doing? Develop the language to articulate your concepts. Others want to know—your loved ones, your kids, your patients, your students, your colleagues, your friends. They want your input and wisdom and guidance. And if you haven't put it together yet, how are *they* going to be able to do so, if they haven't asked themselves the same question earlier? (Remember, it is generally at crisis points in life where these questions come to the fore.) This isn't about religious beliefs per se. This is about discernment, and integrating experience, and listening to your feelings, and using your brain to make a cohesive framework. It isn't about religious creeds or our culture-based images of God. It *is* about our humanity, our recognition of our place and creatureliness and finitude, our resilience and resourcefulness. It is about opening our heart and authentically and powerfully expressing our deepest selves, our own true divine and loving nature. Build up from your religious tradition, whatever it is, and deepen your reverence and awe. This is all about congruence and integration and building upon your foundations. I don't really pay much attention to my clients' belief systems—if it works for them, then it works. But if it doesn't work for them, or worse, if they think it works for them, but the incongruence is obvious to everyone else, well, that's when the process becomes fun and interesting. And I don't ever want to be a functionary again, preaching to the choir. I love the art of preaching. I love reflecting on the teachings in the gospels and trying to figure out how they speak to me, to us, today. I love looking into the collective and timeless wisdom of humanity (which is so much of what the scriptures are all about) and extrapolating how I can better make meaning out of my experiences. But how easy it was, back when I was a parish pastor, to stray into telling others what they should believe or how they should act or what it means to live a moral life. Such pontification was not and is not spiritual care; it so easily becomes anesthetizing, putting people to sleep, shutting down the possibilities for moving into higher consciousness or, worse, inducing guilt and shame. But empowering learning and insight and depth and perspective—that is what is golden.

• And then, *enter in deeply*. Explore realistic potential for redemption, reconciliation, confession and forgiveness, trust, peace, and spiritual security. Do the depth work *with each other*. Go toward the pain, not away from it. Have that talk with your spouse, and with your kids, and with your friends. Become vulnerable and fully transparent. Practice true presence, and create the presence that will draw out that which is unresolved in the heart. And then invite reflection on whatever comes up *from below*, rather than try to fix it somehow from above. Use your higher consciousness to help others access their unconscious. And then move them gently toward higher consciousness themselves.

Illness, loss, trauma, and pain may be awful things, but they are always also an opportunity. It is fascinating to me how so often some people who have done their internal work and have become highly evolved find the wherewithal to respond to loss or an unanticipated change with acceptance, equanimity, and even with a heightened awareness of sacred presence. What a privilege it has been to observe and embrace that process when I've experienced it in others and then to learn from them and facilitate with them true spiritual growth and greater depth of soul.

We do our inner work in order to do our outer work well. For those of us who spend our careers in the helping professions, doing our inner work is absolutely essential. Too many of those in such professions who have failed to do their inner work have become unfortunately famous for acting out compulsively, or worse, serially. Think of all the ministers and celebrities and politicians and presidents who have acted out sexually and abusively. Our outer work becomes the measure of how thoroughly and well we have done our inner work, and is generally recognized as such by others. We know intuitively what it looks like: those people who serve selflessly, who inspire, who lead, who create, who empower. I would suggest that that is, in fact, our natural calling, and it is what is offered to all, without cost, without requirement, without expectation. It is what we are invited into, and the divine spirit both points the way and provides what is necessary, if only we are astute enough and attuned enough to receive it. "Ask, and you will receive; seek, and you will find; knock and it will be opened to you."

When we stop and think about it, an integrated and attuned spirituality looks like this: we manifest centeredness, compassion, gratitude, openness, service, working for justice, being lovers. To quote Eckhart Tolle, "your outer purpose becomes one of awakened doing, and you become one with the ongoing purpose of the universe. Through each of you, consciousness flows into this world. It flows into your thoughts and inspires them. It flows into what you do and guides and empowers you. It flows through you into others and does the same for them."[1] And what are the outcomes? How about these three: acceptance, enjoyment, and enthusiasm for life. The Greek base of the word "enthusiasm," by the way, literally means "filled with the spirit of God," *en-theos*. Acceptance, enjoyment, and enthusiasm. We become filled with the divine spirit. What more could we ask for? And then

---

1. Tolle, *A New Earth*, 293.

just watch as the fear and anxiety fall away, as trust grows, and love rises up. And we feel at one with all things, alive, eternal, beloved.

✻✻✻✻✻

I remember the day so well when one of our long-time obstetric nurses died—it was Maundy Thursday in the Christian calendar, just before Easter, the week of Passover in the Jewish tradition. I had worked closely with her for two years, learning from her wisdom, growing professionally as she shared herself personally with me. She had helped bring into life many babies over the years, held the hands of many mothers in travail, shed many tears at the many chromosomal abnormalities and stillbirths. Her death brought great sorrow to all of us who worked with her. I gathered many of them together in the break room. We spoke of her lovingly, with tears in our eyes. She was one of our "wise ones," and we became aware that her legacy was the wisdom and knowledge that she had generated in those of us sitting around the room. As we told our stories about her and lifted her up, we referenced the ancient Passover story and the Exodus of the Israelites from bondage in Egypt. And we sought the metaphor, comparing the placing of blood on the lintel of the doorway to the blood of the birth canal—the doorway into new life, with all its potential and all its heartache. And the Christian metaphor of what we call *the passion story* came alive in a new way as we expressed our hope that as her painful suffering from the breast cancer came to an end, there was also a release for her, for this beloved colleague and good friend, and there was the ill-defined but so very important hope of something new to come for her, for the two babies that had died the day before, for us all. We all felt deeply saddened but also deeply connected and somehow profoundly borne up, trusting that her spirit would continue to support us and guide us and carry us. As words were spoken and as spirits opened, our tears slowly evolved into poignant laughter and expressions of gratitude. And then the words, "Let's get back to work, we have babies to tend to" from her closest friend, served both as a benediction and an affirmation of life.

We learn to live with a sense of the sacred, with awe and gratitude. Experience teaches us to accept the painful realities of life alongside the wonders, to adapt to changing circumstances with equanimity and trust. As we become more spiritually attuned and intelligent, it seems we become less interested in certainty and more embracing of the mysteries. And the divine spirit seems closer somehow, more engaged with us, intertwined and embedded in our souls, more aligned with our deepest desires for love and nurture and belonging. The great paradox is the more we let go, the more we are filled up; the more we work to empower others, the greater our own energy and voice; the more we seek to heal the world, the more we experience healing and happiness ourselves. Indeed, it all seems beyond belief.

Bibliography

Anderson, Sally. *Free Fall: Living Beyond the Edge*. New York: Morgan James, 2012.

Berry, Thomas. *The Dream of the Earth*. San Francisco: Sierra Club Books, 1990.

————. *The Sacred Universe: Earth, Spirituality, and Religion in the Twenty-first Century*. New York: Columbia University Press, 2009.

Borg, Marcus. *Days of Awe and Wonder: How to Be a Christian in the Twenty-first Century*. New York: Harper Collins, 2017.

Bryce, Marvin E. *Challenge to the Church: A Path to Truth in the Face of Modern Knowledge*. Bloomington: AuthorHouse, 2005.

Buber, Martin. *I and Thou*. Translated by Ronald Gregor Smith. 1923. Reprint, Edinburgh: T & T. Clark, 1937.

Callahan, Daniel. *The Troubled Dream of Life: In Search of a Peaceful Death*. Washington, D.C.: Georgetown University Press, 2000.

Capra, Fritjof, and Pier Luigi Luisi. *The Systems View of Life: A Unifying View*. Cambridge: Cambridge University Press, 2014.

Carson, Rachel. *Silent Spring*. New York: Houghton Mifflin, 1962.

CDC.gov newsroom. *Overdose Deaths Accelerating During COVID-19*. December 17, 2020. https://www.cdc.gov/media/releases/2020/p1218-overdose-deaths-covid-19. html

Chittister, Joan. *The Spirituality of Hope*. YouTube Video 4613. https//m.youtube.com/ watch?v=wk5leyujY8k.

Chittister, Joan, and Richard Rohr. *Prophets Then, Prophets Now*. Amazon.com, Audio CD 1/1/2006.

Dowd, Michael. *Thank God for Evolution: How the Marriage of Science and Religion Will Transform Your Life and Our World*. New York: Viking, 2007.

Eisler, Riane. *The Chalice & The Blade: Our History, Our Future*. San Francisco: HarperSanFrancisco, 1987.

Eliade, Mircea. *The Sacred and the Profane: The Nature of Religion*. Translated by Willard R. Trask. Orlando: Harcourt, 1959.

Ellis, George F. R. *Intimations of Transcendence: Relations of the Mind to God*. *Counterbalance.org*. https://counterbalance.org/ctns-vo/ellis2-body.html?client=ctns2

Fox, Matthew. *Meister Eckhart: A Mystic Warrior for Our Times*. Novato: New World Library, 2014.

————. *One River, Many Wells: Wisdom Springing from Global Faiths*. New York: Jeremy P. Tarcher/Putnam, 2000.

————. *Original Blessing: A Primer in Creation Spirituality.* Rev. ed. Santa Fe: Bear & Company, 1996.

Frank, Arthur. *The Wounded Storyteller: Body, Illness and Ethics.* Chicago: University of Chicago Press, 2013.

Golman, Daniel. *Working with Emotional Intelligence.* New York: Bantam, 1998.

Heschel, Abraham Joshua. *Man Is Not Alone.* New York: Farrar, Straus and Giroux, 1951.

Hillman, James. *Archetypal Psychology: A Brief Account.* Thompson:Spring Publications, 1983.

James, William. *Varieties of Religious Experiences: A Study in Human Nature.* New York: Longmans, Green and Co, 1902. ebooks@Adelaide, 2009.

Janssen, Scott. "A Tale of Two Visitors." *Pulse: Voices from the Heart of Medicine,* 10/23/20, reprinted in the Washington Post, 1/2/21.

Jung, Carl W. "Synchronicity: An Acausal Connecting Principle." The Collected Works of C.G. Jung 8. London: Routledge, 1991.

Kalanithi, Paul. *When Breath Becomes Air.* New York: Random House, 2016.

Kung, Hans. *On Being a Christian.* New York: Crown, 1984.

Leijssen, Lambert. "Grace as God's Self-Communication: The Starting Point and Development in Rahner's Thought." Faculty of Theology Louvain Studies 20 (1995) pp 73-78.

Maslow, Abraham H. *Religions, Values and Peak-Experiences.* Columbus: Ohio State University Press, 1964.

Mohrmann, Margaret E. *Medicine as Ministry: Reflections on Suffering, Ethics and Hope.* Cleveland: Pilgrim Press, 1995.

Moorjani, Anita. *Dying To Be Me: Journey from Cancer, to Near Death, to True Healing.* New Delhi: Hay House, 2012.

Muraresku, Brian C. *The Immortality Key: The Secret History of the Religion with No Name.* New York: St. Martins, 2020.

Nouwen, Henri. *The Wounded Healer.* New York: Doubleday, 1979.

Oliver, Mary. "Messenger." In *Thirst.* Boston: Beacon, 2006.

O'Murchu, Diarmuid. *Quantum Theology: Spiritual Implications of the New Physics.* Rev. ed. Chicago: Independent, 2004.

Otto, Rudolph. *The Idea of the Holy.* Translated by John W. Harvey. London: Oxford University Press, 1924.

Richards, William A. *Sacred Knowledge: Psychedelics and Religious Experiences.* New York: Columbia University Press, 2015.

Schults, F. LeRon, and Steven J. Sandage. *Transforming Spirituality: Integrating Theology and Psychology.* Grand Rapids: Baker Academic, 2006.

Schweitzer, Albert. *The Quest of the Historical Jesus.* Translation by John Bowden et al. Minneapolis: Fortress, 2001.

Snyder, Timothy. "The American Abyss." *The New York Times,* January 9, 2021. https://www.nytimes.com/2021/01/09/magazine/trump-coup.html.

Soelle, Dorothee. *The Silent Cry: Mysticism and Resistance.* Translated by Barbara and Martin Rumscheidt. Minneapolis: Fortress, 2001.

Speth, Gus. Interviewed by Steve Curwood, *WineWaterWatch.org,* 2/13/2015. https://winewaterwatch.org/2016/05/we-scientists-dont-know-how-to-do-that-what-a-commentary/.

Spong, John Shelby. *Why Christianity Must Change or Die: A Bishop Speaks to Believers in Exile.* New York: Harper Collins, 1999.

Spong, John Shelby. *Biblical Literalism: A Gentile Heresy: A Journey Into a New Christianity Through the Doorway of Matthew's Gospel.* New York: Harper Collins, 2016.

Sponheim, Paul. Quoted from a chapel sermon "God, the Whence and the Whither." 1976.

Stone, Emma. "The Emerging Science of Awe and its Benefits." *Psychology Today*, April 27, 2017. https://www.psychologytoday.com/us/blog/understanding-awe/201704/the-emerging-science-awe-and-its-benefits.

St. John of the Cross. *Dark Night of the Soul.* Translated by David Lewis. London: Thomas Baker, 1908.

Swimme, Brian. *The Hidden Heart of the Cosmos: Humanity and the New Story.* Maryknoll: Orbis, 1996.

Tillich, Paul. *The Courage to Be.* New Haven: Yale University Press, 2000.

Tolle, Eckhart. *A New Earth: Awakening to Your Life's Purpose.* London: Penguin, 2005.

———. "You are Not Your Mind." In *The Power of Now.* Novata: New World Library, 1999.

Treffert, Darold. "Genetic Memory: How We Know Things We Never Learned." *Scientific American*, January 28, 2015. https://blogs.scientificamerican.com/guest-blog/genetic-memory-how-we-know-things-we-never-learned/#sa_body.

Tyson, Neil deGrasse. *The Universe,* broadcast on The History Channel.

Updike, John. "The Journal of a Leper." In *Problems and Other Stories.* New York: Knopf, 1979.

Whitehead, Alfred North. "Process and Reality." (Gifford Lectures Delivered in the University of Edinburgh During the Session 1927-28).

Wiesel, Elie. *Night.* Translated by Marion Wiesel. New York: Hill and Wang, 2006.

Wilber, Ken. *A Theory of Everything.* Boston: Shambhala, 2001.

Zukar, Gary. *The Seat of the Soul.* New York: Simon & Schuster, 2014.